Self-Discipline
&
Self-Compassion
2 in 1

By

*Martin Hollins, Peter Meadows,
Kristin Carmichael & Kyle Neff*

Copyright 2018 by Martin Hollins, Peter Meadows, Kristin Carmichael and Kyle Neff- All rights reserved.

The following eBook is reproduced below with the goal of providing information that is as accurate and reliable as possible. Regardless, purchasing this eBook can be seen as consent to the fact that both the publisher and the author of this book are in no way experts on the topics discussed within and that any recommendations or suggestions that are made herein are for entertainment purposes only. Professionals should be consulted as needed prior to undertaking any of the action endorsed herein.

This declaration is deemed fair and valid by both the American Bar Association and the Committee of Publishers Association and is legally binding throughout the United States.

Furthermore, the transmission, duplication or reproduction of any of the following work including specific information will be considered an illegal act irrespective of if it is done electronically or in print. This extends to creating a secondary or tertiary copy of the work or a recorded copy and is only allowed with express written consent from the Publisher. All additional right reserved.

The information in the following pages is broadly considered to be a truthful and accurate account of facts and as such any inattention, use or misuse of the information in question by the reader will render any resulting actions solely under their purview. There are no scenarios in which the publisher or the original author of this work can be in any fashion deemed liable for any hardship or damages that may befall them after undertaking information described herein.

Additionally, the information in the following pages is intended only for informational purposes and should thus be thought of as universal. As befitting its nature, it is presented without assurance regarding its prolonged validity or interim quality. Trademarks that are mentioned are done without written consent and can in no way be considered an endorsement from the trademark holder.

Contents

Self-Discipline 1

Introduction 2

Chapter 1: What Really is Self-Discipline 7

Chapter 2: Getting Started 15

Chapter 3: Your Purpose, Your Mission 45

Chapter 4: Diagnosing Your Self-Discipline Problems ... 62

Chapter 5: Self-Discipline Habits and Routines 76

Chapter 6: Getting Out of Your Comfort Zone 95

Chapter 7: Managing Your Environment 105

Chapter 8: Difference Between Being Productive and Being Busy 114

Chapter 9: The 80/20 Rule 124

Conclusion 129

Self-Compassion 131

Chapter 1: What Is Self-Compassion 132

Chapter 2: Why You Might Lack Self-Compassion 137

Chapter 3: Mindful Self-Compassion 142

Chapter 4: Knowing Yourself 148

Chapter 5: Developing Self-Compassion 152

Chapter 6: Dealing with Emotions 161

Chapter 7: The Power of Self-Compassion 174

Chapter 8: Overcome Your Past 193

Chapter 9: Physiology of Self-Compassion 204

Chapter 10: Putting Yourself Into Action 229

Conclusion 245

Self-Discipline

Mastery of The Mind

Martin Hollins   &   Peter Meadows

Introduction

No matter where you live in the world, it is easy to identify those who have honed their skills of self-discipline. They seem to stand out from the masses regardless of the circumstances. When you have mastered this skill, you know that others will be able to count on you to get the job done right, in spite of any obstacles you may face.

The US Navy SEALs, one of the world's most elite fighting forces live by the mantra, "Pain is Weakness Leaving the Body." It's no wonder that people everywhere view them with deep respect. Sadly though, few people can actually say that they have mastered this quality of self-discipline to this extent. While it is highly desired among so many, the number of people who can follow through on a plan in spite of negative circumstances are minimal at best.

Most of us may believe that we are not capable of living up to the kind of commitment that self-discipline requires. However, there is not only a good reason for you to embrace the possibilities for mastering this quality, but there is also a good reason to do so. While it is a desired trait in many, it is not an inherent trait; we are not born with this ability to control our actions. That means it is learned behavior, which by extension, means that the ability to master it is within all of us.

Having self-discipline is not the same is having motivation. When we are motivated to do something, we are eager to tackle the project. We will easily forego eating, socializing, or spending time on our favorite activities when we are motivated. However, when we have to tackle a job that we are not motivated to do, the circumstances are different. We may sincerely want to accomplish the task, but something gets in the way; we are easily distracted, and it seems almost impossible to push through the drudgery.

Why Everybody Needs Self-Discipline

After years of research, the true secret to success has finally been uncovered. Those who are most successful in life are those who have mastered the power of self-discipline. In other words, they are able to push through those kinds of activities that no one else wants to do. When they have a workable goal in front of them, they are willing to do whatever is necessary in order to achieve their desired results.

It doesn't matter what your goals may be, if you're not disciplined enough to work through the dull and boring parts of the task, you will not achieve success. This involves ignoring the temptation to watch your favorite TV show, the ability to not answer the phone when you're deep into a task, or saying no to that dinner invitation when a deadline is on the line

It doesn't matter who you are, self-discipline is an important quality to have in every aspect of life. When you have it, you have the power to follow through on all of your decisions without sidestepping responsibilities. It allows you to persevere through the thick and thin of any circumstance, and it builds in you an inner strength that you can apply to overcome addictions, avoid procrastination, avoid lazy tendencies, and resist instant gratification. You'll also learn to:

- ❖ Control your impulses
- ❖ Fulfil promises and commitments made to others
- ❖ Follow through on a project long after the enthusiasm has faded
- ❖ Stick to your diet or exercise regimen
- ❖ Get up on time
- ❖ Or anything else you want to do

Through the pages of this book, you will learn the little secrets that will help you to master success by building up your own self-discipline. Together we will discover:

- ❖ What self-discipline really is
- ❖ The fundamental elements of self-discipline

- ❖ The ways in which having a purpose can lay the groundwork for good self-discipline
- ❖ How to identify your own weaknesses when it comes to self-discipline
- ❖ Why it's important to step out of your comfort zone
- ❖ How to take control of your environment
- ❖ And much, much, more

You will understand how to use discipline in your day to day life, and fundamental routines to apply that will steer you in the right direction, no matter what your goals are.

How to Use What You Learn Here in Your Daily Life

To get the most out of the lessons included in this book, it is important that the strategies and tactics listed here serve more than just reading fodder. You need to apply them as soon as possible. When it is recommended that you take action, then do so, whether you understand it fully or not.

You should set a goal right now to succeed in mastering your self-discipline before you turn the page. That will set the precedent for the entire book and get you in the right mindset for success. Don't hesitate as that will automatically put you into procrastination, which will set you back on your goals even before you get started.

You are not a spectator in your life, so you should make it your goal to be an active participant in the exercises included here. Have fun with it, experiment, and see nothing as an impediment to your goals but rather see them as a stepping stone to your future. Once you've achieved that mindset, there will be nothing that can stop you from mastering your own level of self-discipline.

There are plenty of books on this subject on the market, thanks again for choosing this one! Every effort was made to ensure it is full of as much useful information as possible, please enjoy!

Chapter 1

WHAT REALLY IS SELF-DISCIPLINE

There are many ways to define self-discipline. Most of us understand it to be the ability to regulate one's actions to accomplish a set goal. Some people may give a simple answer in explaining it. They may say it is self-control, the ability to restrain oneself, or an exercise in willpower.

While all of those answers are correct when describing self-discipline, its true definition goes much deeper than that. When you have self-discipline, you have the ability to push through difficult and challenging things in the hopes of achieving a goal of improving yourself in the end. The skill can be applied to any aspect in your life. Whatever your goal, it is the ability to do whatever it takes to achieve it, no matter what.

All of us have some form of self-discipline but we each may possess it to a different degree. However, we can improve our degree of self-discipline simply by understanding it better. Most people think of it as a matter of willpower, the action of making a decision to follow through on something and seeing it to its end. To a certain extent this is true, however, we are all biological creatures and it helps to understand the science behind what is happening internally when you exercise self-discipline.

The Biology Behind It

All of our behaviors originate in the brain. Scientists have long understood that this organ is made up of 100 billion neurons that work together to produce our thinking and our conduct. While we have learned a lot about how the brain works, there is still a lot of uncovered territory, so you can fully expect that what we have already come to understand will be expanded on in later years.

However, based on research completed to date, we have come to learn a little bit about how the brain processes the thought patterns that surround our self-confidence. Through the use of functional magnetic resonance imaging machines, they have been able to observe brain activity as it happens while people are exercising their self-discipline.

Through these studies, it has been observed that the ventral medial prefrontal cortex experienced an increase in activity when participants were asked to make a choice between accepting a large monetary reward for some time in the future or a smaller reward now. The old age battle of whether or not they could delay their gratification.

A second area of the brain that fired when such decisions were presented is the dorsolateral prefrontal cortex. This is the area known to function when trying to decide on future options. When the participant of the study was weighing long-term consequences, there was a much higher degree of activity in this region of the brain.

From these studies, researchers were able to determine that the type of self-discipline needed to make these kinds of choices were much easier for some people than it was for others. The difference was due to the amount of activity and the structure of their prefrontal cortex. Through this, they have been able to determine exactly what part of the brain is responsible for decision-making and self-discipline.

This information coupled with the realization that the brain is a constantly learning machine which helps us to understand that contrary to what we used to believe, it can be trained to change habits. The old phrase "you can't teach an old dog new tricks," does not apply here. The ability to learn self-discipline is within all of us. So, if you are that individual that has a hard time saying no to people or resisting things you know are bad for you, take heart. With the right training and understanding, you can develop this skill and reclaim your power of decision making, giving you much more control over your life.

So, what makes one person's level of self-control different from another? It is understood that a part of your development in this area is genetic in nature, but not all. So, while some may develop this skill easier than others it does not mean that those who struggle with it cannot work to build it up to the same level. A good portion of your ability to master this skill comes from your environment and how you were raised in your home. We cannot say with confidence, that one person has the ability to master self-control over another person based entirely on genetic. All of us have the ability to improve our actions over time so that you can achieve the degree of self-discipline you've always wanted.

The Power of Self-Discipline

The ability to be delayed or wait for gratification can be a very powerful skill to master in your life. It means that you will be able to set goals and muddle through all sorts of obstacles until you actually achieve them. This requires an intense level of focus, shutting all types of interruptions out that may otherwise distract us. It means being willing to wait for things you want with the hope of getting a larger payoff in the future.

It also gives you the ability to narrow in and concentrate on what is more important, not just for today but also for the future. Your ability to set priorities will automatically give you more control over your life and avoid knee-jerk or impulse reactions to events happening within your environment. In other words, you learn how to slow down and meditate on the consequences, which can be both empowering and motivating.

The more you are able to slow down and get the big picture of things, the easier it will be to find workable solutions to the problems you face. You know how to evaluate the pros and cons and decide on an effective resolution that has a better chance of success.

According to a study published in the Journal of Environmental Psychology, conducted with a group of girls from several Chicago neighborhoods, it was determined that the greater a girl's self-discipline, the better her chances of performing well in school. The more likely she would avoid getting involved in risky behaviors or picking up unhealthy habits. As a result, she was more likely to achieve success in the future.

While there may be many books published on the secret to success, take the time to look at each of them and you'll find one underlying principal in all of them. You have to train your mind to be more self-disciplined. By doing so, you give yourself the power to achieve the goals you set out to do and have a great deal of success waiting for you if you do.

Self-Discipline vs. Instant Gratification

Many people are now familiar with the infamous Marshmallow Study that was conducted back in the 1960s. At the time, Stanford University researcher Michael Mischel gave us evidence that connected self-discipline to success later on in life. By taking a group of 4-year-old children and giving each one a single marshmallow he gave them a choice; to wait for another marshmallow when the interviewer returned or to be happy with the one they had.

The results of the test were quite profound. Some of the children immediately took the single marshmallow and indulged themselves, while others delayed their gratification and waited for the second marshmallow. At the time of the study, the results didn't tell very much about the child's development, but it revealed a lot fourteen years later when the same children were called back in.

By then, they had already graduated from high school, and that's when the real results became apparent. Those children who were able to wait for that second marshmallow were found to have a more positive outlook on life. They were self-motivating and persistent when faced with difficult challenges. In fact, they were able to delay their gratification until they had successfully pursued their goals. For all intents and purposes, these young adults had developed habits that would put them well on their way to being successful adults. Their future looked bright and they were prepared for better marriages, better careers, and even better health.

On the other hand, those children who could not wait had a more troubled future ahead of them. When they were evaluated years later, they were found to be more indecisive when it came to serious matters, tended to be less confident, lacked trust in others, and still were not able to delay gratification when something more enticing came along. They were more easily distracted and often lost their focus when studying. This lack of control over their minds and their lives if not corrected was expected to put them on a path that led to low job satisfaction, poor health, and an overall dissatisfaction and frustration with their lives.

The evidence from the study underlines the same principles that apply with all of us. Our sense of self-control is going to be tested throughout our adult lives. It's no secret that putting off the things we love to do will be painful at times, but it will be well worth our while if we can stick to it. This is not to say that every time we delay gratification we will be successful, but the odds are definitely in our favor if we can learn to not live our lives entirely by impulse reactions. Once we master the skill of taking our time, developing a plan of action in each situation, our odds of success increase exponentially.

What You Can Accomplish With Self-Discipline

The evidence is overwhelming, self-discipline is usually the key element that leads to success. You'll be able to make practical decisions and control your emotions at the same time. Your behavior will be more stable, and you'll stay focused longer, so you can strive to achieve more meaningful goals.

That does not mean, however, that you must live a life of deprivation, eliminating all types of enjoyment from your world. Nor does it mean living the life of a pauper or malcontent either. To become self-disciplined is not the same as depriving yourself of fun but it can give you the freedom to learn how to channel your mind and your energies so that they are trained on your goals. It means developing a mental attitude whereby you control your actions and make deliberate steps towards your end goal.

In short, by mastering the art of self-discipline, you will accomplish a more orderly and stable lifestyle that will lead to a much more satisfying life.

Chapter 2

GETTING STARTED

Before you can work on your self-discipline, you need to be aware of where you are starting. You are about to effectively start sculpting your inner self but if you don't know who that is, it will be very hard to meet this challenge. Throughout your life, you will have to face many battles but the one that will be the most difficult is the battle that is constantly pushing and pulling within yourself. You need to first learn how to get your mind and your body working together on the same goals.

Throughout your life, you will face many challenges, some you will expect and others you won't. While you have little to no control over what happens externally in your life, to overcome these obstacles you'll need the perfect blend of discipline and patience to see things through. If you can learn to take the time to develop an actionable plan before you do anything, you won't run the risk of self-sabotaging your efforts and undermining your goals.

However, to do this, you have to be able to identify those habits that are often getting in your way. Once you have been able to identify those hurdles you can take an active approach to eliminating them so that they no longer prevent you from following through on your plans. To do this, you need to know where you are going.

If you're about to venture into an area you've never gone before, it can be very challenging to do without a map. You know where you are right now, but you must have a specific destination in mind. Once you know where you want to be, you can chart a course that will lead you directly there. So, the first step in creating your road map is to start with the fundamentals.

Start With the Fundamentals

You have to start at the very beginning. You, like many other people, automatically assume that you know yourselves. It's part of human nature to expect that we understand ourselves better than others, but the reality is more often the opposite. So, before you can begin, you need to push aside all those preconceived notions about who you are, what you really want, and what you can do. I can guarantee you that your opinions about those matters are far less than what the truth really shows.

Through several years of research, it has been discovered that while no one always gets their way in any given situation, there are those who think they always can.

Those people are usually the ones that had parents that gave into their every wish growing up. When parents cater to their children, especially at times when the brain is developing, the children fail to learn the importance of controlling their inner urges or even taking the time to consider long-term consequences. The end result is an individual who has not learned discipline or the pillars of self-discipline.

However, even as an adult, this pattern can change. One must start by developing their own ability to focus on what's important. Since focus is one of the primary factors of self-discipline, it is a good place to get started. Your ability to focus directly correlates to your discipline. It is completely dependent on something researchers have termed executive functions.

Executive functions are primarily responsible for five important skills:

- Focus
- Organization and planning
- Initiating tasks and seeing them through
- Controlling emotions
- Self-monitoring

Let's talk a little about the first one: focus. There are three elements that when able to function together allow you to focus. First, is your working memory, your ability to control your emotions (impulse control), and cognitive flexibility. When you exercise these elements, your brain is able to set goals for you to pursue, prioritize your life, filter out any distractions, and control all of your impulses at the same time.

Now, that we've learned that the brain is responsible for these functions, we can work towards increasing the blood flow to it as a first step in improving our ability to focus. But how can you do this? There are several approaches you can take.

Meditation has been known to help people increase their ability to focus for centuries. For years, this was questioned by many who doubted its ability to have any genuine effect on an individual. However, MRI scans were taken of participants in one particular study before starting a course on meditation and a separate one afterwards, the results showed that it has been very effective in strengthening those areas of the brain that are key to focus.

In addition, it was shown that it can literally shrink the amygdala, which is the part of the brain that is responsible for our instincts, emotions, and survival mechanisms. This is where our internal fight or flight responses come from. Those who participated in tone study were asked to practice meditation for a period of eight weeks. The results showed that at the conclusion of the study, they were found to be less likely to succumb to fear or have those instinctive reactions when under stress.

In addition to that, the results also showed that the brain's gray matter of the prefrontal cortex and the anterior cingulate cortex actually became denser after meditating. These are the areas of the brain that are responsible for self-regulation and cognitive flexibility. This is evidence that meditation can boost your ability to control your emotions and physically improve the areas of the brain that are responsible for them.

So, one of the first things you need to do to develop your self-discipline is to carve out a period of time in the day to take in some meditation or mindfulness practice. You don't need to carve out a lot of time for this. Consider adding just a few extra minutes to your morning routine or at another time of the day when you are less active.

While your goal is to enhance your self-discipline, it cannot be done if you're not able to focus. The two are completely interrelated. If you cannot keep your mind trained on your long-term goals, then your discipline won't be of much use to you anyway.

Another area you need to pay attention to is your willpower. Closely related to motivation, you have to protect this quality at all costs. Your body is a biological instrument that needs to be constantly refueled. We often think of refueling in the sense of making sure we have nutritious food to eat, but our body also needs to have other things refueled besides food and drink. When you use your self-discipline or your willpower, it is like taking cash out of your savings account. If you are constantly making withdrawals and no deposits, it is just a matter of time before your account will be depleted.

What does this mean? Simply that there is not an unlimited source of willpower in your body to rely on. Given enough temptation, the pressure will eventually win out if you don't protect it. Studies have shown that most people are able to resist temptation once in their life. But a repeated onslaught of pressure will eventually weaken your resistance. There is much scientific evidence that shows that the brains of those who have resisted temptation once are distinctively different from the brains of those who've had to resist the same thing ten, twenty, or even a hundred times.

Regardless of how well you've resisted in the past is not proof that you won't give in at another time. Each time the pressure is put on, the brain's ability to resist is weakened a little if you don't work to replenish your willpower. While physiologically, we can do without life's essentials for a time, when we deplete those things we rely on for survival, our brains will automatically switch to a survival mode, which will automatically switch over to instant gratification, which is the last nail in self-discipline's coffin.

Your best defense against such reactions is to ensure that your brain never reaches that point. You do this by avoiding challenging your willpower unless it is absolutely necessary you're your best to stay away from situations that might cause you to use them. For example, if you're on a diet, constantly putting yourself in a bakery or a place with foods that will hamper your goals is going to challenge your willpower more than necessary. Until you build up your resistance to those things, it is best to stay away from temptations if at all possible.

Everything is Interrelated

There are four key fundamentals to self-discipline. They are basically just four different habits that can effect just about everything in your life. You may have known about these fundamentals in the past, but never connected them to your ability to control your actions. They are:

- ❖ Sleep
- ❖ Nutrition

- ❖ Movement
- ❖ Meditation

These four fundamentals make up the foundation of nearly everything you need to lead a healthy lifestyle. Once you master these, you'll be fully equipped to maintain control of your life. You will be calmer, more focused, and have more energy.

You've probably already seen this in action. Have you ever noticed how different the behavior is of a person who doesn't get enough sleep? They tend to be more irritable and difficult to please. However, a well-rested person is calmer and much more focused.

What's most interesting is that all of these fundamentals have an effect on all the others. When one goes off kilter, you can expect the others will be off too. For example, if you are capable of sleeping well every night, you wake up with good energy to get through your day. You'll eat better, which will give you the energy to move. That in turn, will help you to meditate, which will give you a calmer state of mind so that you can sleep.

On the other hand, if you wake up in the morning without getting enough sleep, you are already low on energy. Your survival mode kicks in and you start to have all sorts of cravings, which cause you to take artificial stimulants to keep you going. You make unhealthy eating choices, which causes your blood sugar to spike (or crash), and you run out of energy. Without that energy, your mind cannot focus and you're unable to meditate and you go off to bed completely out of control, which could cause you to have another bad night's sleep. To build up self-discipline, you need to start with these four fundamentals.

Pick a Foundation Habit

It can be very tempting to try to tackle all three at once, but it is better to ease into this new change. Just pick one habit to start with and build from there. As we've said, they are all interrelated so once you master one, the others will quite likely fall right into place. Start with the one that presents the biggest challenge to you. By focusing on that one, you'll create a nice little ripple effect that will almost instantly have an impact on your life.

We'll talk about each one, in turn, so you can decide which one will be your biggest challenge to overcome. For each person, the main element will be different. While some people won't be able to get a good night's sleep, others may have trouble getting nutritious food to eat. Whatever is your biggest challenge that will be where you begin your journey to self-discipline.

Sleep: You may be surprised to learn that it's only been in the last 150 years that we get as little sleep as we do. Up until 1879, the average person slept ten hours a night. However, with the invention of electricity and the light bulb, daylight hours can be extended all night if we want to. This means that our periods of activity were no longer limited to when the sun was out. As a result, our sleeping habits gradually started changing. With each successive generation, our sleep time became shorter and shorter. Today, the average person sleeps only seven hours a night and some are only getting around six. This means that the majority of the world is already sleep deprived.

Throughout the years, numerous sleep studies have shown that even a small percentage of sleep deprivation can have a negative effect on how we function throughout the day. If you want to get control of your behavior, then getting good quality sleep is absolutely essential.

It is important to realize that losing an occasional good night's sleep will not have a lasting negative effect on your body. However, if you habitually are deprived of sleep it will have a definite impact on how well you function. Sleep deprivation is cumulative. If you're only missing a few hours' sleep a night, you may not see much of a change at first but over time, you'll notice that you'll fall asleep at odd times during the day. It will be hard to keep your focus on tasks and the condition will get progressively worse.

The average adult needs to have 7-9 hours of sleep every night. Sadly, we live in a world where sleep is a luxury that most of us can't have. Our lives do not leave much room for rest, so you need to maximize your sleep time as much as you can. If your body is not getting enough sleep, you'll notice the telltale signs if you look for them.

If you fall asleep instantly when you lie down, or you need an alarm clock to wake you up in the morning, chances are you are already sleep deprived. If you find yourself hugging your pillow and not wanting to let go of the covers in the morning, or you're feeling tired and listless throughout the day, these are clear indications that you need more sleep in your life. You already know the feeling when you've had a good night's rest. You wake up full of energy and you can usually maintain that alertness all throughout the day.

So, how can you make sure that you're getting the right amount of sleep? Here are a few tips you can try.

- ❖ Make sure your bedroom has the right environment conducive for sleep. It should be dark, absent of any kind of light. Light tells your brain it is time to be awake and prevents the body from releasing the

hormones needed for sleep. The darker your bedroom the more comfortable you'll sleep.
- ❖ It should also be cool. Ideally, the temperature should be set between 65-70F.
- ❖ It needs to be quiet. Remove the TV from your bedroom, it should be a haven where you can find peace and quiet. If there are other noises that seep through your bedroom walls, drown them out with either white noise or a good fan, which can also help in keeping the air circulating, aiding in a better night's sleep.

It is also important that your daily habits are in line with your sleeping patterns. A lot of what you do every day could inhibit your ability to sleep at night. If you're a regular caffeine drinker, this may be what is causing you to lose precious sleep. Consider making these adjustments to help you extend your time sleeping.

- ❖ Restrict your caffeine intake to morning hours only. Many people do not realize just how long caffeine stays in your system after you drink it. If you're going to have caffeine in your diet, then try to do it as early as possible in the day. Anything you consume in the afternoon or evening should be decaffeinated.

- ❖ Also, consider limiting your physical activity to earlier in the day. In fact, you should avoid doing any extensive or highly strenuous physical activity less than three hours before you plan to sleep. When you are very active physically, your body's core temperature increases, and it will take time for it to drop. Your core temperature is the temperature of your vital organs. When it is too high, it causes the blood vessels in the skin to dilate so that heat can escape. It also causes you to sweat, as it attempts to get the body to cool down. If the temperature is too cold, the blood vessels will constrict to conserve heat. Ideally, your core body temperature should be somewhere between 96.8 and 100.4 degrees. Your body can sleep only if the core temperature is low. When the temperature is high is when you are energized and fully awake. Taking steps to lower your core temperature can do wonders for helping you to sleep better.
- ❖ Another activity that few people think about is their eating habits. When you eat, your body has to generate more energy to digest your food. Eating just before bedtime makes it more difficult to relax and fall asleep. Avoid eating or drinking anything but water for at least three hours before retiring.

❖ Quit smoking. We all know and understand the myriad of health problems that are associated with tobacco. Many people have the habit of having a cigarette before sleeping, but they do not realize that the nicotine in their system actually has a negative impact on their ability to sleep. Nicotine causes the heart rate to increase so you will feel more alert when you're trying to relax. This fast-acting drug enters your blood and can reach your brain in a matter of seconds and it can take hours before it starts to leave your system. During that time, even if you do sleep, it is not a restful sleep that will refuel your body and prepare you for the next day.

Once you've applied all of these steps, you'll begin to notice that you will be able to sleep much better. However, you don't want to stop there. You want to make sure that you develop a consistent sleeping schedule and do everything you cannot to stray from it.

First, determine exactly how much sleep you need each night. Start by trying to get to bed at a time that will allow you to have between 7.5 to 9 hours of sleep. You will discover your optimum sleep quotient when you can wake up feeling refreshed without the aid of an alarm clock or someone to rouse you then you have found your personal sleep quotient.

Stick to that sleep pattern by getting to bed every night at the same time. You'll find that even on the weekends you'll be happy to crawl into bed so that you can enjoy that valuable and highly rejuvenating form of sleep. When it comes to stabilizing your internal sleep patterns, you will need to be consistent.

Finally, start a pre-sleep routine by preparing your body and mind for sleep. The last hour before you retire for the night should be peaceful. Turn off all electronic devices (yes, that includes the TV, computer, and cell phones) and do something that will relax your mind. This could be taking a hot bath, listening to quiet music, or just going back to the old-fashioned activity of reading.

Nutrition: Another physical element that could be affecting your self-discipline is keeping your nutrition in check. We have often been told that the foods we eat are fuel for the body, but we need to also understand exactly how our dietary habits affect us on a daily basis. While good nutrition is important for everyone, as we get older it becomes even more important. We need to find foods that will replenish our bodies, encourage good health, keep us alert, and supply us with energy so we can function well throughout the day.

Poor eating choices often have the opposite effect. This is why having a balanced diet will help to improve your ability to control your daily habits. You have probably heard of the saying, we are what we eat. That means that the foods we consume are the building blocks of who we are as a person. If we want to have healthy practices in our life like good self-discipline, then we need to give our bodies healthy fuels.

But, what is a healthy nutrition plan? Every day, we hear of many experts who weigh their opinions on what is good or not good for you. Some say cut out sugar, others say reduce fat, others say that carbs are the enemy, and still others are watching for salt. It can literally be overwhelming to decide who is right and who is wrong when you consider just how much contradicting information is out there to sift through.

Rather than sifting through all the expert opinions, it is best to stick to the facts, those that have been proven to be of benefit to your health, supported by studies and documented proof of their effectiveness. With that in mind, here is what we know about creating a balanced nutrition plan.

1. Your diet needs to include both macro and micronutrients so that it gets all the essentials it needs.
2. You need to keep your calories down to a reasonable level
3. Avoid eating processed foods or those containing harmful chemicals
4. Try to eliminate trans fats and excess sugars

No matter what diet you choose to have, if you keep those basics in mind, you should see your overall health improve. Make sure that your diet includes a healthy dose of:

- ❖ Green, leafy vegetables because they contain most of the vitamins, minerals, and fiber you need.
- ❖ Include colourful vegetables and fruits like carrots, squash, tomatoes, bananas oranges, etc. These contain many of the vitamins and potassium your body needs.
- ❖ Learn to use onions and garlic when you cook. They protect the body from inflammation and infections that may be caused by bacteria or viruses.
- ❖ Many kinds of beans can give you the essential minerals and protein you need.
- ❖ Nuts and seeds offer you a good dose of protein and healthy fats.

- ❖ Proteins can be found in different types of fish and poultry. Limit your red meat consumption because they have been known to lead to other health problems.
- ❖ Healthy fats are essential in any diet. You can get these from sources like olive oil, avocados, walnuts, and sunflower seeds
- ❖ Make sure you are drinking plenty of water every day. This should be your primary source of rehydrating your body. In addition to water, consider drinking black coffee, or tea and limit your intake of sugary drinks and alcohol.

This can be a major adjustment for most people so don't try to do it all at once. If you try to make these changes all at once at best, you will be successful for a short period of time but eventually, you'll tire out and give up. It is best to make this type of adjustment gradually, so you don't become overwhelmed.

Start with making one small change each week so your body will have a chance to adjust to the new form of nutrition. You might start by eliminating one bad food each week and replacing it with a good food. For example, you might start by having a little fruit with your breakfast and eliminating sugar from your meal. Keep making this type of adjustment until you reach the point where you're having a healthy breakfast every day and then start working on perfecting your midday meal.

Another thing you need to consider is your portion control. This is just as much a psychological practice as it is a physical one. To avoid over eating consider taking these little steps.

1. Use smaller plates. If you simply switch from a 12-inch plate to a 10-inch plate, you'll automatically eat 22% less.
2. For drinks, start using taller glasses but make sure they are slenderer. Our brains will see the added height and will think you are getting more when in fact, you are getting about 20% less.
3. Remove unhealthy foods from your line of sight. Make sure that your more nutritious choices get primary visibility in your home.

By making a more gradual switch to these new habits, it will be much easier to manage your new nutrition plan. Managing your nutrition is just as much about controlling your environment as it is about making the right choices for what to put in your mouth.

Get Moving: Another way to get more control over our bodies is through regular movement. When you think about it, it has only been in the last few generations that we have lived a very sedentary lifestyle. Even our regular activities are often spent in a seated position. Most of us work behind desks, our entertainment is often things like going to the movies or a restaurant, and at home, we spend countless hours fiddling with our devices and gadgets. There's not much motivation for movement in our lives.

Our ancestors, who have the exact same DNA as we have, spent their days running, climbing, jumping, lifting, and dancing as part of their everyday life. We have to find a way to put all of that back into our daily routines. Your body has more than a trillion cells and every single one of them is uniquely designed to recognize movement. That means that everything you do will work towards helping your body to function better. When you include regular movement in your life, your immune system works better, and so does your reproduction and digestive systems. When you don't get enough movement, everything begins to slow down including your self-discipline.

This doesn't mean that you now need to start spending endless hours at the gym. Of course, exercise is definitely a form of movement, your life is capable of incorporating movement into your everyday activities. You can decide to walk to your local store rather than drive, take the stairs to your office rather than the elevator. Add a few stretches throughout the day to elongate your muscles so they work better. As long as you give your body the movement it needs every day, you'll start to see a difference in how your mental functions perform.

This does not mean that you can't incorporate exercise in your life, but while you may exercise for an hour a day, you won't see much of a change if the rest of the day is completely sedentary. The movement should be a part of your regular life whether you exercise or not. If you are exercising regularly, you'll see a lot more results if you have a steady stream of movements to give you more balance.

The more movement you can incorporate in your daily life, the more biological changes will occur in the brain. As you embark on your goal to improve your self-discipline, you will need that extra brain power to help you master the steps. When the brain learns to adapt to new things, it must make new connections to do so. Movement stimulates the brain to release more positive neurotransmitters (dopamine, serotonin, and norepinephrine) which are essential for brain development. In addition, the movement also boosts the brain's production of the protein BDNF, which encourages more growth of branches that carry messages from one neuron to the next.

For years, we have understood how important movement is for the physical body, but we are just now beginning to get a clearer understanding of how the brain is affected by it as well. Imagine how much better control you will have of the thought processes needed to improve your self-discipline if you have added just a little more movement into your life.

Again, you do not have to make a major change in this area. Start small by making tiny little movements and then grow from there. For example, every time you prepare a meal in your kitchen, you could place essential foods in the highest cabinet, so you will have to stretch and reach for them every time you need them. Or, if you work at a desk, consider changing your sitting position every fifteen to twenty minutes to work on new muscles.

After incorporating these smaller movements into your daily routine, you can then start adding in larger movements. Consider doing a few fundamental exercises with a morning warmup routine. You might be able to do a couple of sit-ups or pushups before you start your day. Get a pedometer, and start building up the number of steps you take each day. Then you can move your movement up to another level by incorporating even more physical movements like dancing, yoga, Pilates, or running on a regular basis.

There are countless ways you can incorporate movement into your daily routine. In the beginning, you may struggle with this until it becomes a habit. You may have to add this to your schedule until you reach a point where you can do it automatically. And, you can manipulate your environment to encourage more movement until you get the hang of it.

- ❖ Park further away from your destination
- ❖ Place things you need on a regular basis out of reach
- ❖ Consider walking when you're on the phone with someone rather than sitting down

The key here is to loosen up the body with more movement so that you can stimulate your brain. Don't stop with the basics. As you master more movements keep looking for other ways you can move your body in order to encourage better brain function.

Meditation or Mindfulness: Your brain is a machine that never turns off. Even when you're sleeping the brain is still working, filing information you've accumulated for the day, creating dreams for you to decipher, and regulating vital organs that need to be functioning to keep you alive. Meditation can be a way to give your brain a valuable rest.

If you try, for just one minute to think about nothing for even a few seconds you'll find it is literally impossible.

Your mind doesn't know how to stop working. This phenomenon is referred to as "mind chatter"; there are always things going on the background. As soon as you stop actively thinking about what's concerning you, new thoughts will begin to emerge.

However, while you can't turn off the mind chatter, it is possible to quiet it down but to do that you need to understand what is really happening in your mind.

Two Minds

Most people are aware that the mind is not just a simple stream of thoughts flowing through it. While that is definitely part of it, there are two things happening at one time. First, your conscious mind is busy figuring out what you're going to do at work every day, deciding on what you're going to prepare for dinner, and probably worrying about whether or not your boss is going to discover the mistake you made yesterday. This is often referred to as the 'thinking mind.' Few people realize though that there is also another mind that is also constantly at work, called the subconscious mind or the 'observing mind.'

When your thinking mind is active, it is nearly impossible to control it. You pass a bakery on the street and the aroma can automatically send you back in time to your grandmother's cooking. You hear your favorite song on the radio and you're back to your wedding day. Any subtle suggestion may send your thoughts in one direction or another before you realize it. It doesn't matter if you want to think those thoughts or not, they just appear without warning and no matter how hard you try to reign it in, those thoughts will continue to reappear until something else comes along to distract you.

Interestingly enough, the same can be said of our emotions. The thought enters our head and before you know it, the emotions follow, so if you're having negative thoughts about something, guess what? You're going to trigger negative emotions from them. So, what can we do to stop the onslaught of negative thoughts and emotions that may be dictating our behavior and causing us to lose self-control?

The reality is clear, if we want to get rid of negative feelings (anger, jealousy, fear, and sadness) then we have to start doing something about changing our thinking pattern. We've already said that we can't control the thoughts that flow through our minds, they pop up unbidden at the most inopportune times. However, we can learn to control how we respond to those thoughts when they appear, in essence, through meditation, you can learn to not feed into them.

It used to be that many people thought that meditation was the practice of emptying the mind of all thought, but now that we understand that is impossible, we have a much better understanding of what happens. It's not about stopping the flow of thoughts running through our minds, but it is the act of channeling our observant mind to focus on our thoughts in a very specific way.

When you meditate, you actually boost your metacognition or your ability to analyze what you are thinking. The better you are at this, the easier it will be to not allow those negative thoughts to pull you in. You strengthen your observant mind by becoming more aware of what is happening both in your mind and body. As you get better at this, you'll be more aware of what is happening in your mind and body and will be able to respond to it better.

There are many benefits to regular meditation. First, regular meditation can actually shrink the amygdala, the part of the brain responsible for fears and emotion. At the same time, the prefrontal cortex, the part of the brain responsible for your sense of awareness, concentration, and decision making (all qualities needed for self-discipline) gets thicker. Just like physical exercise can strengthen your muscles, meditation strengthens your brain function.

When it comes to self-discipline it can have a major effect. When you use meditation to calm those involuntary emotions, you do not take your thoughts and feelings too seriously. You learn to see your thoughts from an external perspective. Then you can identify it and move on. In essence, you learn that negative thoughts are not a reflection of reality but are more likely your brain creating scenarios that have not and may not ever happen.

Once you understand that thinking is not the same as reality, it becomes much easier to keep negative feelings in check. You can then learn to identify a problem and take the time to make a better informed choice. When you do this, you will start to see that you have a more controlled pattern of behavior and you'll be in better control of your actions.

How to Meditate

There are many different ways you can meditate. Your goal is not to find the right way to meditate but instead, to find a form of meditation you can do and make it a daily habit. Here are a few basic guidelines to help you get started.

- ❖ Make it simple. There is no need to find the right position or to chant a particular phrase or to sit perfectly still for any length of time. You can start first by sitting in a chair and observing your thoughts for one minute. From there you can extend the amount of time and get more involved as you progress.

- ❖ Decide on when you will meditate. Some people prefer to practice it in the morning when their mind is fresh while others try to do it in the evenings. There isn't an exact right or wrong time to meditate. You can choose to do it after breakfast, before breakfast or any other time of the day. The key here is to choose a time and stick to it, make it consistent so that you can develop the skills and practice.
- ❖ Find a quiet place. When you meditate you want to be in a place free from distractions. Find a place you can escape to for a couple of minutes without being disturbed.
- ❖ Find a comfortable position. Some people are perfectly comfortable in the lotus position, but you don't have to sit that way. You can choose to sit on your sofa, on the floor, or in a chair. The position is not as important as comfort. If you are not comfortable while meditating, you won't be able to stick with it for long.

Simple meditation is just taking the time to observe the thoughts running through your mind as an outsider. Once you start doing this, you'll be surprised at the thoughts that are controlling your emotions. When you can identify them, you can choose a completely different approach to how you react to them, which is the first concrete step toward better self-discipline.

Recognize that many of those thoughts are not reality and once you realize that, they will lose their power over you. Compare what is going on in your mind with what is real, and you'll know what decisions are right to make.

You can meditate on every aspect of your life but in the beginning, it might be best to just select one or two habits you want to focus on changing. When you concentrate on specific habits, you are practicing mindfulness, another form of meditation.

For example, you might want to work on your ability to wake up at a certain time every day. In the mornings, you might lie in bed and focus on the sounds outside when you wake up. The more your brain focuses on these things, the more your body will be able to respond to those cues to rouse you from sleep in the morning.

You can use mindfulness to concentrate on improving your eating habits. By focusing on the meal in front of you rather than watching TV or talking on your phone you will become more aware of the foods you are taking in. This will lead to making better choices when it comes to good nutrition.

Mindfulness can also play a role in how much exercise you choose to take in. Take a walk sometime, concentrate on your breathing and your surroundings. Start focusing on your environment and before long, it won't feel much like exercise any more. You'll learn to appreciate the things around you and it won't bother you to be outside in them.

As with all the other suggestions made so far, ease into this. Start simply and build up gradually. You might feel bored and uncomfortable at first, but as your observant mind begins to reveal more things to you about yourself, you'll find the exercise that much more interesting.

Chapter 3

Your Purpose, Your Mission

Now that you have prepared your mind for better self-confidence, it is time to prepare the heart as well. Through countless years of study and research, we have learned that the brain never stops growing. This next section we're going to talk about what also happens in the brain, but we refer to it as heart work since it deals more directly with how we feel about things.

There are two kinds of mental processes that directly connect with your attitude about something. You can have a fixed mindset, which means that you believe that your personality and individual qualities are fixed and that they cannot be changed. On the other hand, the growth mindset means that you believe you are a person who is continuously developing and that your unique traits can be changed or adjusted over time.

As you can see, if you want to boost your self-discipline then you need to have a growth mindset. Throughout this book, you will be asked to make certain changes in your life, but if you have a fixed mindset, you may start to make excuses. That's just the way I am, or that's my personality, I was born with it. This type of attitude will definitely get in the way of your ability to make the necessary changes required to enhance your self-discipline.

There are other challenges for those with a fixed mindset They may feel that they constantly have to reinvent the wheel in order to convince themselves and others that they have the ability to do something. Whereas the growth mindset, removes that need entirely. Your personal view of how you interact with the world will be full of completely new experiences at every turn. You won't expect to be perfect because you see everything as a new learning experience. You're more likely to take on more challenges, will continue to pursue certain goals until you have achieved them, and won't get discouraged in the face of setbacks. You will find something new in every experience and will understand that you don't need to be perfect every time you try something new.

There is a huge difference between the two. However, if you have a fixed mindset, it doesn't mean that you can't change, you just have to believe you can. If you don't get to the point where you believe it is possible, you won't take the necessary steps to try the strategies listed here or to develop other skills you want to master in your life.

Only you know if you have a fixed mindset or not. If you do, then the first thing you need to do is change your belief system. Think of some of these facts:

- ❖ The brain consists of 100 billion neurons each of which has about 50,000 connections to other cells to transmit your thoughts on things you already know and are learning.
- ❖ This means that the number of connections between all the neurons in your brain actually exceed the total number of atoms in the entire universe.
- ❖ The neural pathways this creates in your brain are constantly changing

After you have meditated on those numbers think about your age and how much you have learned in your lifetime. Do you honestly think that your brain has reached its maximum capacity for learning during those years? You have the most advanced learning machine at your disposal and all it needs is for you to put it to use. Your brain's learning power is without limits; it is only what you believe in your heart that puts the brakes on your ability to make changes.

If you already have a growth mindset, then you can skip the next step, but it is my guess that most of you will stay right here and follow the instructions. Even with the growth mindset, there are times when you may doubt your abilities, and this is a great way to remind yourself that you can do more than you believe. At the same time recognize those things that cause us to doubt our ability to make changes when we meet with certain obstacles.

Go back to your meditation sessions where you learned to observe your thoughts. Whenever you need to face a new challenge that you're not sure of the outcome, negative thoughts will flood your mind. Take note of what those thoughts are; you will know that they come from a fixed mindset voice telling you that the goal is not possible.

Whenever these thoughts come up, remind yourself that you have a choice. You can opt to believe your negative voice, or you can ignore it altogether, and apply the strategies to see what results you get. You can even talk back to yourself, have an internal dialogue where you work to convince yourself of the possibility. As you continue to challenge those negative inner thoughts, your belief system will begin to crumble making room for more empowering and positive thoughts to come in. Now, you're in a position to take action and start working towards your goal.

Finding Your Purpose

You've heard the expression, a jack of all trades and a master of none. The easiest way to reach one goal is to focus on one thing at a time. The person who tries to do too many things at one time rarely does anything well. When your thinking is scattered, it is difficult to focus on what is important, which can be very limiting, frustrating, and discouraging.

This requires a little bit of modesty on your part. The person who is willing to accept the fact that they can't do it all will find they have reduced much of the stress they've invited into their lives, and they are better able to focus on the task in front of them. This doesn't mean that you can't one day achieve everything you set out to do but being realistic enough to admit that you can't learn it all at one time.

So, your next strategy to improving your self-discipline is to narrow down your focus to a manageable size. Ask yourself these questions:

- ❖ What do I enjoy doing?
- ❖ What kind of things am I good at?
- ❖ What are people willing to pay me for?

When you have only one goal to reach, you have no fear of dividing your time among many different things and can focus all of your energies on pursuing that one particular goal. This is the exact type of focus needed to kick-start your self-discipline in the right direction.

As you make your list, you'll find that many of your answers will overlap. For example, if you love to cook, are good at it, and people are willing to pay you for it you will have all three elements involved in that one skill. This would serve as an incentive to develop that skill. Now, let's talk about this in a little more detail.

What do I enjoy doing? There are many things that we enjoy doing. Most of us love listening and dancing to music, sports, traveling, or just spending time with our friends. You can end up with quite an extensive list of things you really enjoy doing but having a passion for those things is not enough. You may love to dance but if you're not good at it, you won't be able to parlay that into something people will be willing to pay for. This doesn't mean that everything you pursue has to be a money making venture but adding that extra element could be the key to boosting your self-discipline later on.

What kind of things am I good at? While your first list will be quite extensive, this list will narrow down your options a lot more. Often times, when you're really good at something you may not even realize it right away. These talents usually come quite naturally to us and we just view them as a part of life and not as any particular strength or skill.

You may need the help of someone close to you to assist you with this aspect. You could also take a few personality tests like the one found at 16personalities.com that may help you to narrow your focus through several free online tests. These types of tests are surprisingly accurate and can reveal a lot about you that you never knew before.

What are people willing to pay me for? While your goal may not be to get paid for something you love to do, it does help you to get a real view of how the rest of the world will value the skills and talents you hope to develop. What kind of people you will be able to help and how you can use those skills in relationships with others.

When you're narrowing down your focus, make sure that the area you want to target first in your self-discipline program is on all three of your lists. This way, you will be sure you're getting involved in a major part of your life and not a mere hobby or personal interest. By doing this exercise, you can narrow in on your focus and actually find your purpose in life. It's a win-win situation that will boost your self-discipline in many ways.

What do You Want to Accomplish

When it comes to self-discipline, the biggest challenge is finding out how to stay out of your own way. You are engaging in a battle against yourself. It is you that is holding you back from the things you want to accomplish. One way to prevent this from happening is to fine tune your awareness of your ultimate goals.

When a Navy Seal is sent out on a mission, they are faced with obstacles at every turn. Some of these challenges will be known before they set out others they won't know until they are face to face with them. They are fully aware that they are unable to control every situation they will go into and can fully expect that somewhere along their path someone is going to try to stop them.

So, what makes a Navy Seal's self-discipline so strong? They know exactly what they set out to accomplish before they start. They know to expect the unexpected and they are prepared to use their training and discipline to get them to their end result. You have to approach your life with the same mental mindset. Having a clear end goal in mind can be a powerful tool in keeping you on track and avoiding many of the tricks of self-sabotage.

When you have a clear-cut goal in front of you, it is much more difficult for you to be distracted. You will be better equipped to see just how you are getting in your own way and you can develop strategies to avoid those practices or remove them altogether. It is impossible to achieve a goal if you never set one. You must first decide exactly what you want out of life and then use it as a guide for every decision you make. Whether your goal is to make more money or to lose weight, it is your mental preparation that will help you to develop your self-discipline habits and fuel your motivation.

Think like a Navy Seal. They don't quit something because they meet an obstacle; they anticipate challenges and develop a game plan that allows them to adapt their approach whenever necessary. However, it all starts with their knowing the end before they start.

This all starts with "why" you do what you do. No matter where you are starting on this venture, you are reading this book to make a change. That means that somewhere inside of you there is a "why" that you have to bring out. Take some time to give this some serious contemplation. Once you have identified your why and connected it to a bigger purpose you'll find more of an incentive to keep pushing ahead in spite of the obstacles you will inevitably have.

Preparing Your Mind

Most people who lack self-discipline are usually applying their will power arbitrarily. Take a dieter for example. They apply their will power at the beginning of the diet, excited to see results. But, after a few weeks with little to show for their efforts that will power begins to wane and temptations will easily distract them. At the heart of this mental preparation is your motivation.

All of us have some level of motivation, but we don't have it in infinite supply. Therefore, we need to look internally again to find out just what is our motivating force so we can tap into it to help us achieve our goals. When we are more motivated, our bodies have more fuel to push forward in spite of obstacles. In order to maintain optimum levels of motivation, even among the most passionate of people is to know exactly what moves you to take action.

Before we can do that though, we need to define what motivation really is. The word comes from the old word 'motive', which means an internal need, want, or desire that stimulates people to action. When you feel motivated, your body generally feels excited about what is to come. Sadly though, most of what we need self-discipline for is not in the least bit exciting. So, we have to discover ways to motivate ourselves when the things we need to do are not as attractive as we'd like them to be.

If you know your 'why' you now have an anchor that will ground you and give you the energy and the desire to push through the challenges you face. The 'light at the end of the tunnel' can become a powerful motivating force to pull you through.

It is important to not gloss over this point. Many people will automatically say that money, fame, or power are at the seat of their motivation. They feel that if their bosses wanted to give them more money, more recognition, or more exposure then they would definitely push harder to achieve their goals. On the surface, this may seem like the obvious motivator in everyone. However, research has shown that these things are not at the heart of real motivation.

While people may say that they want power, money, control, etc. these are only good for short-term motivation. What really fuels the hearts of most people is the need to be validated. Many people who want power may actually want more autonomy and freedom to do what they want to do.

Those who want more money may secretly desire to acquire the things they believe only money will bring them. Keep in mind that there is a good chance that your first thought about motivation is not usually the right one, but if you examine it more deeply, then you will likely uncover the real reason you are inspired to do things.

There are two different types of motivators: intrinsic and extrinsic. Extrinsic motivators are those that are dependent on external events to meet them. Your boss giving you a raise, the movement of the stock market, or your wife remembering your anniversary. Intrinsic motivators are those that come from within you and are usually based on your individual needs and wants.

As you self analyze, keep in mind that your awareness of these motivators and how you use them are the key to improving your self-discipline. We all need the basic essentials of life and if you're lacking in any of those things they can be powerful incentives to push through to better times. However, once we have the basic essentials in place, our motivators turn more internally. We are then driven by the need for personal fulfillment, pleasure, and satisfaction in life. This may mean working overtime to pay for that vacation you want or pushing hard to build a strong relationship with others. What's most important at this point, however, is that you know what motivates you, so you can use it to fuel your self-discipline.

Getting the Right Mindset

Another way you can prepare your mind is to define your limitations within a certain area. You might be a proficient chef and know how to prepare hundreds of delicious dishes, but that does not mean that you have to be an expert in Chinese, Arabian, French, and Swedish cooking. You have to define what you are realistically capable of and stick to that realm.

Take Julia Child's for example. Everyone knows her as a world-famous chef, and while she has tried to prepare many dishes from around the world, she is most known for her French cooking. The same can be said of Martha Stewart, she has narrowed down her focus to an area of entertainment that she is most comfortable with.

Each of us has a unique body of knowledge in areas we feel we are an expert in and limited knowledge in other areas. Your success is not dependent on knowing every tiny bit of information in your particular area, but you can define a specific niche that you are expert in, which will give you a unique perspective as you pursue your goals.

None of us are perfect and our efforts to be the one person who knows everything and is expert at all will have us spinning endless wheels that will delay our ability to achieve success. The more effort you put into pursuing your goals rather than trying to achieve the impossible the more confidence you'll gain and the better self-discipline you will have.

How Your Brain Works

It is clear that many of us lose our self-control because we have little to no idea what our goal or our purpose really is. That is only part of the problem though. Another huge part of it is in how our brains really manage our impulses and our will power. While this research is still in its very early stages, we have learned some very valuable clues to help us understand ourselves better.

Let's take losing weight as an example. When we are trying to lose weight, we have to make many different choices on what to eat. But the brain is not thinking in terms of this is good and that is bad. Instead, it is processing historical data you have previously fed it. This is healthy and that is not, or this is good for my health and that is not.

It is obvious which decision will be most beneficial, yet responders generally fall into two different groups. Even though many are aware that ice cream is not the best choice when on a diet, they will still opt taste over health. This is because the ventral medial prefrontal cortex gets involved in such decisions as it is responsible for making value judgments in the mind.

There is another area of the brain that also gets involved. The dorsolateral prefrontal cortex, which can sway the decision by influencing the other part of the brain. When these two parts interact and work together, people tend to have stronger self-control as they can balance each other out. It seems that the relationship between the two regions suggest that we all have some awareness of our self-control abilities before a decision is made.

The question then becomes, do we have the ability to change how our brain is working when we demonstrate a lack of self-control? While there is no drug that can stimulate the two parts to work together, it is possible that one's inability to demonstrate self-discipline could be related to other drugs we may be using.

Neurologists have learned that while all of us use the same area of the brain to make decisions based on these values, there is a second region that works more to govern and modulate the activity of that section of the brain. In other words, one area of the brain makes the decision, but a second area of the brain supervises it and exercises a certain amount of control over it. This second area inserts more abstract factors that apply to the given situation into the equation.

This knowledge helps us to understand how self-control actually is produced in the brain. It can also give us some insight into how the decision making process gets involved. The key then is to strengthen that area of the brain that is responsible for overseeing the process of making decisions, but regularly going beyond basic likes and dislikes and inserting the abstract concepts that could affect a decision.

For example, when weighing decisions based on whether something is healthy or not, developing defensive strategies to help us avoid looking for the easy way out could be the secret. Imagine a dieter choosing between a healthy food and one that is unhealthy, cauliflower vs. ice cream. The obvious choice for good health is cauliflower but the preferred choice among most people would be ice-cream.

Since most people do not like cauliflower, a dieter may choose to replace cauliflower with a more neutral food rather than the two obvious choices; tomatoes and avocadoes, for example, will help them to balance out their dietary needs without the feeling of guilt. Over time then, they can gradually build up their resistance until the point where they will choose cauliflower over ice-cream because they will be making their decision based on health rather than on what tastes better.

Chapter 4

Diagnosing Your Self-Discipline Problems

Now, it is time to get a little personal here. As we have already said, everyone has some level of self-discipline. Think of the child that doesn't want to eat his vegetables; no amount of logic or reasoning, and in some cases, punishment can get him to deter from that drive. Self-discipline is plentiful in all of us when it is something we genuinely don't want to do. However, the challenge we all face is to channel that same strength of will to areas where we are less inclined to show resistance.

That kind of discipline is what is needed if you ever hope to accomplish those big goals you have for your future. All of us have an internal desire to improve our lot in life, but it's our lack of self-discipline that often throws us off the path to our destination. When that happens, we often blame others for our own failings. The economy is bad right now, there are no healthy food choices here, my boss doesn't want to give me a raise. While all of these may have some degree of truth the reality is that if we were truly determined to reach that goal, none of those issues would have stopped us.

The degree of self-confidence you have determines how easily those excuses will knock you off your chosen path. You, like many other people, may not even realize just how you yourself are contributing to your own diversions. To understand this better, you need to take a cold hard look at your day-to-day life and learn the ways you have self-sabotaged your efforts in the past. You will be surprised to learn just how much of your own actions are influencing just how you react to those external obstacles. While others may be getting in your way, it is quite likely that your own internal thoughts and habits are contributing to your lack of self-discipline just as much.

What's Getting in Your Way

Unrealistic Goals: One of the common obstacles that can get in the way is to set ourselves up for failure from the very beginning. We have dreams bigger than any of us are truly capable of and we may set out with the best of intentions, our enthusiasm is high, but the unrealistically high expectations will eventually get the better of us and we will start to taper off and fail.

When we set our goals, we don't usually take into account our regular habits and routines. We picture ourselves at the end of the journey and not as we are pushing through it. This gives us a lot of hope in the beginning, but when we meet with the first resistance, we quickly peter out and fall back into our regular bad habits.

As one psychology professor, Peter Herman explains, when we strive for the extremes, we have not truly understood the difficulty of the challenge ahead. While we may begin with a lot of enthusiasm for the project, we cannot sustain that momentum, which will inevitably lead to failure. In the beginning, you may have a clear understanding of what you want to accomplish, but you have not prepared yourself for the challenges you face as you strive to reach them. This clarity begins to fade in the face of adversity and will be replaced by all those tempting things you find hard to resist. In the end, your goals will be pushed aside as you opt for things that are more comfortable and easy to deal with. Remember, our bad habits and poor self-control will not go away simply because we will it. You will have to be proactive when it comes to changing bad habits and it won't happen overnight. While you want to set positive goals for yourself, you want to always keep the goals within the realm of possibility and to do that, you need to be self-aware of what is feasibly possible and what is not. This does not mean that you can't achieve the impossible. But your goals should be set in reachable stages, so you can not only imagine your success but also plan ways to overcome the obstacles you will inevitably face.

Procrastination: Another self-sabotaging tact we may not be aware we are using is procrastination. Many people may find that they are fully capable of accomplishing certain tasks but will put it off while they wait for the perfect conditions. A writer doesn't want to commit to the work ahead of him because he's waiting for inspiration, a runner chooses not to run because it might rain, or a worker puts off his project because he is waiting for the right tools.

The problem with all of these scenarios is that none of them will stop you from accomplishing your goals. They may have the ability to slow you down, but running is still running, whether it's raining or not. There are often excuses that you allow to convince you that a task cannot be done unless conditions are ideal.

This is a fairy tale picture of real life but is not a true expectation of how the world works. Nothing will ever make up the perfect combination of experiences and those conditions will never really exist. Even if all the elements to accomplish a certain goal are right in front of you, it is only a matter of time before something else will come along and derail your efforts.

This doesn't mean that you won't have doubts about your work; this is just human nature. You will have to find a way to strike a balance between the enthusiasm for the project you want to achieve and those internal nagging doubts about your chances of success. However, if you never start, putting off for that moment that will never come, you will never receive the chance to pat yourself on the back and give yourself that well-deserving and edifying well done.

One way to combat this tendency is to apply what is called the 75% Rule. Basically, it means that all things considered, you should start working towards your goal when you have reached 75% preparation. When you come to realize that you will never reach that 100% level, you'll start to see that the 75% point is a much more realistic option.

Just deciding that you are going to be more disciplined rarely works. It is a habit and it can only get stronger if you choose to exercise it, so the sooner you realize that you need to get started to improve your self-discipline you will be less inclined to procrastinate on future goals.

Rationalization: Speaking of patting ourselves on the back can also be a way of self-sabotage. Some of us have a tendency to sit back and relax once we have already achieved some goals. We congratulate ourselves a little too much and feel like now is the time to reward ourselves rather than push on to the next goal.

It is always good to accept recognition for a job well done, but we are never finished with life until we are literally finished with life. Simply achieving one goal should not be the end of what we want for ourselves. Remember, we are not working for a destination, but we are living the journey. If you spend too much time relishing in your past successes, you will get the feeling that you don't have anything else to do. This will cause you to rationalize and come up with reasons why you do not need to take the next step.

To control this self-sabotaging behavior, you first need to recognize what is happening and intercept that thought process. It doesn't matter how much you feel you deserve a break, stop yourself from rationalizing or it will slow down and maybe even stop your progress completely. Each stage in your life needs to stand on its own merit. You may have received 5 stars from your kindergarten teacher when you were five, but those stars don't mean a whole lot when you're standing in front of a board meeting with an unprepared presentation. Whenever you catch yourself thinking about your past accomplishments and feeling like relaxing, this is the time when you need to kick-start your self-discipline.

If you can master identifying this characteristic in you and stopping it as soon as it starts you will be able to see even greater accomplishments in the future. You won't find yourself stalling in your attempts to reach your goals and you'll learn how to persist through many other obstacles you will meet later on.

Parkinson's Law: Closely related to procrastination is Parkinson's Law where people often claim that they can only work when they are under pressure. This can, in fact, be true in some cases. The phenomenon is known as the Parkinson's law, which states that as long as you have a deadline, the amount of work you have to do is going to fill that time frame. In actuality, you create a condition that forces you to draw on your personal self-discipline. If you have a tight deadline, a time crunch so to speak, the only way to meet it is to use your self-discipline.

The theory was named after a British historian by the name of Cyril Parkinson. He noticed this pattern in those within the British Civil Service. It seemed that their efficiency levels increased or decreased based on the type of deadlines they had to meet. The more time they had to perform a task the laxer they became in their work.

The way to overcome this natural phenomenon is to always set yourself tight but realistic deadlines. You want them to be close enough to challenge you but not so far into the future that you would be tempted to allow other things to interfere with your progress.

Being able to diagnose what is getting in your way will require you to take a close personal look at yourself. Let it be a warning to you, once you turn your eyes inward you may not always like what you see. Many realize that they have been their own problem all along. Once you are able to identify exactly what your self-sabotaging habits really are, you can develop a strategy to circumvent them and not allow them to have control over your actions.

Keep in mind that you are working on discipline. Just like your child is not happy when you exercise discipline on him, much of the strategies you develop will feel uncomfortable at first. However, if you push through them and make the necessary adjustments in your life, you will begin to see real progress in how you manage your self-discipline.

While there may be external obstacles that get in between you and your goal, most often they are obstacles. How you react to them is what will make the difference. You can view them as an obstacle and decide to go around them, or you can use them as stepping stones and go over them. The real problem is often the tricks we play on ourselves and you can only fix those when you can identify them and develop a strategy to either avoid them, go around them, or bulldoze your way through them.

Knowing Your Strengths and Weaknesses

We fully understand that discipline is not supposed to be pleasant, so it is understandable that you would not be inclined to inflict discomfort on yourself. It is a means of self-correction when we start to go astray. We learn discipline mostly from our environment. Your parents may tell you not to touch a hot stove when you are young, but the majority of us will do it anyway. Not because we want to be disobedient but because we are curious. However, once we have touched that stove and been burned, the words of our parents ring that more soundly in our ear.

No matter how much you think you know, understand, or believe, any type of discipline is going to be uncomfortable. This is a basic fact of life. So, to be able to endure the punishment you will inflict on yourself, you will need to fall back on your own inner strengths and weaknesses. By relying on these internal resources, you will be able to accept the discipline, learn from it and grow.

This will play itself out as a mental exercise. When you first begin exercising, it can be difficult, almost impossible, but as your body gets stronger, that discomfort begins to feel more like a small annoyance, which will eventually develop into a stronger self-discipline. So, what inner strengths and weaknesses do we have and how can we use them?

When you know your own unique inner strengths, you have a built-in power you can leverage when things get tough. Those strengths you have can become the tools you use to push through those difficult and uncomfortable periods when you're struggling, but you can't use them if you don't know they are there and within your reach.

According to the book What You're Really Meant to Do, most people have very little knowledge about what their strengths and weaknesses really are.

To identify your personal strengths, think about the things that come the easiest for you; the things that require little or no effort for you to manage. For example, you may find it easy to strike up a conversation with strangers, or you may be able to think on your feet in stressful situations. Here is an exercise that might be able to help you.

First, make a list of five qualities that you find extremely easy and comfortable to do. List them in order with number one being the absolute easiest for you and number five being the most difficult. Now that you have a physical piece of paper in your hand, take a close look at your list, you can start to visualize ways you can rely on those strengths to pull you through the tough times when your discipline may seem to be failing.

When you've finished your strengths, do the same with your weaknesses. These are the things that can get in your way and hold you back. Identifying them makes it easy to think of ways that you can work on to help you to improve. Start making strategies that will help you to improve these weaknesses and be able to identify them when they get in the way of you accomplishing your goals. When you know your strengths and weaknesses, you have a much better understanding of the kind of person you really are, and you can create a platform that you can grow from.

As you work on your self-discipline, you may think that it is better to give more attention to your strengths than to your weaknesses, but you will need them both. When you rely on your strengths you are creating more opportunities for yourself and thinking positively about your goals. When you focus on your weaknesses, the actual act of improving them will help to build your self-confidence, which will naturally give you a psychological advantage and help with your self-discipline.

How to Avoid Problems

By tapping into your inner qualities, you develop a strategy that will help you to avoid the problems that sometimes get in the way of meeting your goals. Discipline is something that has to be applied no matter what the circumstances are. It doesn't care if you are tired and exhausted, nor does it matter what the weather is or what other people think. In fact, when those conditions are present, you need to rely on it the most. But beyond the inner qualities you use to your advantage, here are a few more suggestions that can help you to get past the challenges.

Many of our regular habits are actually addictions so we need to shed our bad habits in much the same way as you would cut back on a drug habit. When the urge to stray from your chosen path comes up, recognize it as an addictive habit that needs to be broken. Urges do not come on in a constant stream; they come in waves. They first may appear as an idea that increases in intensity until it reaches a peak and then it will gradually subside. If you stand still in the water as the wave increases, it will crash down on you and maybe sweep you away, but if you manage to lie down and ride with it, it will gently carry you into shore where you can get back on your feet and try again.

Learn to identify those urges. Recognize them for how they make you feel, the sensations that flow through your body, and the emotions you connect with them. Once you recognize this sensation coming again, go back and apply some of those meditation techniques you learned earlier. Focus on your breathing and then let those feelings pass through you until it passes.

It is natural to give into something that is so strong when it hits us but being able to understand that these feelings do not last forever and will eventually subside makes it possible to ride it out to the end. When you are riding the urge to the end, you are not really battling against the desire that you have to do something or to push through on something, but rather the feelings that are associated with it. If you are able to identify and separate the two, you will find it much easier to let the urge pass and end up back on your feet.

Depending on what you have the urge for, it can last anywhere from twenty to thirty minutes before it subsides. Learn how to ride through them rather than fight them off. If you are successful in doing this, the strength of these urges will eventually subside, and they will have less power over you, making them easier to control. That's one point for your self-discipline and zero for the urges that come on.

Another way to battle the temptations to go against your discipline is to learn to get comfortable with discomfort. This is a common theme of the Navy Seals. When they are facing battle, the only thing they can truly rely on is their self-discipline. They have the drive to stick through a plan even when things do not turn out the way they expected. If their self-discipline fails, they are not the only ones to lose; mistakes are made and lives are lost. At best, every time they go out on assignment, it is a true test of their self-discipline.

Navy Seals, therefore, learn to live by the phrase "get comfortable being uncomfortable." A Seal has no idea when he goes out whether he is going to have to face the extreme cold, dodging weapons across dangerous territory, or any other oppression that he might face. He knows that he will be uncomfortable before setting out. But he has mentally prepared for that discomfort before he takes the assignment. He has learned to accept this feeling and use it as a way to increase his self-discipline, so he can best prepare for his enemy when he faces them.

Now, no one starts out with the strength and the fortitude to be a Navy Seal. These qualities are developed through intensive training and hard work. At one time, all Navy Seals were just like any one of us, proving that building your self-discipline is a skill that is found in all of us, we just have to tap into it and practice it the same way they did, regardless of what your goals may be.

Chapter 5

SELF-DISCIPLINE HABITS AND ROUTINES

Becoming self-aware is key to identifying the bad habits that may be derailing your self-discipline. If you want to reach your goals, you need to also develop the good habits and routines in your daily life that promote a healthy level of self-discipline. Aristotle once said, "Good habits formed at youth make all the difference." Perhaps you didn't form those habits when you were young, but there is nothing stopping you from developing them right now, today.

If you study the lives of many successful people, you will find that all of them have one thing in common. They have developed and practiced good habits throughout their lives. They may have started on a rocky plane, but they didn't achieve their status until they reigned in all of those bad habits and put forth the good ones. Here are some good habits you should start cultivating in your life right now.

Remember when we talked about those neurons in the brain. Habits are simply those actions that we have done so much that the brain has developed a personalized neural pathway to access every time you do it. This is what makes our behavior automatic. When we exercise a habit, the brain no longer has to think about it, allowing the mind to focus on other things it's not so familiar with.

So, while these habits may not be easy to do in the beginning, after consistent repetition, we will master these as our neural pathways related to them become stronger. So, by incorporating these good habits and routines in your life, you will start to see your self-discipline getting stronger. You won't see instant results, but if you are persistent, start small and build on them, you'll eventually begin to see progress. Some of these habits may not even seem to be related to self-discipline but they are all connected in some valuable way.

Practice Gratitude: When we are grateful for things we have, we are less likely to satisfy that urge for instant gratification. It takes us a step away from always wanting more of what we don't have. Take the time to appreciate all those around you and even the little things that they do.

The benefits of gratitude are probably more than you might imagine. It has not only been able to boost our mental health, but it also encourages us to be more balanced emotionally, and spiritually. Gratitude, over time, helps us to feel like we have an abundance even when we are living with limitations.

This applies also to those who may be suffering from physical problems. Anytime the physical body is not functioning the way it was designed to do, it produces stress hormones, which can inhibit our abilities even further. This interferes with our digestive, immune, and reproductive systems in a negative way and we end up feeling worse than we really should.

To practice gratitude, start by taking at least 10 minutes every day noting down all the things you are thankful for. This doesn't have to be limited to physical things, but it could also be abstract things as well. Are you thankful for your family, the sunrise, your health, friends, even the food on your plate? If you can't think of anything to be thankful for, then take a closer look inside of you, there is always something, you just have to dig a little deeper to find it.

Be Forgiving: Whenever we interact with other people, it is only natural that you're going to reach a point where one is going to be offended, feelings hurt, or someone otherwise will have caused you to develop negative feelings. Anger, regret, resentment, and guilt are often behind all of the conflicts that we face every day. These negative emotions start to eat away at much more energy than anything else you might do. However, when we learn to let those feelings go, we can also let go of the energy that has our self-discipline in a vice-like grip.

Being forgiving clears our mind. Think about the last time you were angry with someone, what were you thinking about? Likely your thoughts got stuck in an endless repetition of the offence and you could think of nothing else. This doesn't mean that you have to approve of the wrong done to you, but you no longer allow that offense to take control over your mind because when it controls your mind, it will affect the whole body.

Forgiving means letting go of the negativity that zaps our strength. It is also an excellent exercise in self-discipline because usually in the beginning it is painful to let something hurtful go. We all innately want to be right and we want justice, but most of the time, the things we want are completely out of our control. So, we find ourselves spending endless days, weeks, months, and even years waiting for an opportunity to set things right for us. Look at how much of that time is wasted when we could be focusing on more important factors in our lives.

One way to learn to be forgiving is to try for a minute to think like the other person. Take the time to meditate on the wrong you were faced with, but look at it from the point of view of the other person. Think about what you would have done in the same situation, then look at it as a third neutral party. Is there a humorous story to tell? Is there a lesson to be learned? It is much easier to forgive someone if you come to understand them better.

Get Organized: Organization is also an excellent habit you need to develop self-discipline. In actuality, they are deeply intertwined. If you are organized it feeds your self-discipline and if you are self-disciplined it feeds your organization. Apply this habit in both your professional and personal life. This might be very difficult to accomplish at first so start small and build on it.

You can start by focusing all of your attention on one aspect of your life and when you have developed that into a good habit, then add another element. You can start by getting your bills organized, then move onto your kitchen cabinets, your desk, your daily schedule and so on. If you work on it and build each phase as you would any habit, it will pay off in the end.

Manage Your Time Better: We all have the same 24 hours in a day, but some people seem to handle a heavy workload better than others. This is because they have better time management skills. When we can manage our time well, we seem to find more room for the things we want to do. We can then include activities that will allow us to achieve our goals and do the things we thought we didn't have the self-discipline to do.

Think of the experiment performed with filling an empty jar with rocks (the things you have to do) and sand (the things you want to do). If you put the sand in first, then chances are you won't be able to put all the rocks in too; they just won't fit. However, if you put the rocks in the jar first, then you will be able to get all the sand in as well, letting it fill up all the empty voids of your life. View the rocks as those things that are urgent, and you absolutely have to get done and the sand as all the things that you really want to do.

When you have a task to do, rather than approach it haphazardly, try to develop a system that will prioritize what needs to be done.

- ❖ Short-term Crises and Problems
    Important and urgent
- ❖ Long-term Strategic Goals
    Important but not urgent
- ❖ Distractions and Interruptions
    Urgent but not important
- ❖ Time-wasting Activities
    Not important and not urgent

You can see from the above list if you categorize your workload in a similar way, then the first and the second list will require more attention than the last two. Based on this guideline, you can decide exactly what needs to be prioritized first and what can be put off until later. Once you've made your schedule then you have to develop a strategy to help you stick to it. The more you do this, the easier it will be to get things done more efficiently.

Be Persistent: As you build up your good habits, expect that you will hit a few snags along the way. Let's face it, if it was easy then everyone would have the kind of willpower and self-discipline you're striving for. Persistence is the mental state of mind that won't let you give up, even if you fail, it will pull you back up on your feet so you can try again.

Setting goals is hard, achieving them is hard, but getting discouraged and giving up is easy. You need to learn how to push through, even if it is uncomfortable until you reach a point where it will give you pleasure. Expect failure but don't look at it as a failure, view it as a stepping-stone that will redirect your steps in the right way, so you can achieve your goals.

How to Develop and Teach Yourself Good Habits for Self-Discipline

Teaching yourself good habits can be a challenge. It is not as easy as saying "I'm going to do that from now on." If we could do that then we wouldn't need to learn self-discipline. However, there is a very simple formula that will help you to set up a good habit system that you can rely on until the new habit becomes a regular part of your life.

There are four fundamental parts that will help you to understand exactly how to build a new habit and reinforce it in your life.

- ❖ Cue
- ❖ Craving
- ❖ Response
- ❖ Reward

Understanding each of these parts can help us to use them as tools to build up a good battery of habits we can rely on to build up self-discipline.

The Cue: The cue is a trigger the brain receives in order to initiate a specific behavior. The brain recognizes this cue and understands that if it triggers the preferred action, there is a reward waiting. The rewards can be anything that validates the action. Most of us perform certain actions because we want the obvious rewards, money, fame, power, status, praise, approval, friendship, and love. The brain is constantly analyzing its environment for cues to where we can accept these rewards.

The Craving: The next step in building habits is the craving. This is the force that motivates the action of every habit. Without something to motivate us, we would have no reason to take any action. You're not craving the habit, but you have a craving for the change that the habit will produce. You turn on your TV not because you want to turn it on but because you're craving entertainment.

Every person has a different craving. Anything could trigger a craving, but whatever triggers your craving is completely unique to you. So whatever cues you have are meaningless until you give it a value. So, it is your thoughts, emotions, feelings, and beliefs that can take a cue and turn it into a craving.

The Response: This is the actual habit that you want to cultivate. It is the action you take when you receive the craving. The stronger your motivation the more likely you are to take the necessary action. The more effort an action requires the higher the motivation you will need to launch an adequate response. It also depends a great deal on your ability to perform the task. It can only become a habit if it is something you can do. If you want to become a baker, you need to have the skills and materials to do it.

The Reward: The reward is the goal you set for yourself once you've mastered the habit. Going back to step one, the cue tells us that there is a reward, the craving is your motivation for the reward, and the response is how you get the rewards, and finally, the reward is received. Without a reward, developing habits is virtually impossible. This doesn't mean that the reward has to be great. It could be something as simple as a word of praise or a hug from a family member, or it could be something bigger like a bonus paycheck, a vacation, or a new car.

We pursue rewards because they both satisfy us and they teach us. The primary purpose for a reward is to ease the craving. Food and water, the two biggest rewards serve us by giving us the energy we all need to live. Promotions give us money and respect, and exercise improves our health. It is the reward that stops the cravings and brings us relief.

Through rewards, we also learn which habits are worthwhile in pursuing. Your brain is designed to seek out rewards of all kinds from the environment. Since they tap into the pleasure centers of the brain, a reward that brings pleasure will automatically encourage the brain to repeat, but a reward that offers disappointment will see a decreased level of motivation the next time a cue is triggered.

While the reward is at the heart of all four phases of habit forming, if any habit you are trying to develop is unable to deliver on any of the stages, it will not develop. Without the cue, you will never get started, without the craving and you won't want to do it. If the habit is too difficult you won't be able to do it, and if there is no reward, there is no incentive.

To successfully develop new good habits all of these elements need to be included. Each of these four steps creates a neurological feedback loop that will allow you to develop these lifelong habits.

If you want to take this a little further, you can divide these steps into two phases: the problem and the solution phases. The first two steps, cue, and craving, can be viewed as part of the problem phase where the brain is recognizing a problem it has to solve. The second two steps, response, and reward, are the brain's way of working out that problem. All behavior triggered in the brain is designed to solve a particular problem. You may not see it as a problem, but your brain does. The role of the habit is to solve whatever the problem is.

This process should not be something that you do when you find the time, but it should be a continuous process that doesn't stop as long as you are developing the habit. It needs to be done until you are performing these actions without actively thinking about them. Most of our habits we learn as children and never give a second thought to them. Think about some of the habits you do every day, such as:

- Turning on a light switch
- Brushing your teeth
- Eating
- Going to school
- Driving a car

All of these are learned behaviors that were developed through the four-step process. All of us have hundreds (if not thousands) of habits we have developed over decades that we perform without any thought whatsoever. From the clothes we choose to wear to how we go shopping, we are all performing habits.

By taking these four fundamentals, we can use these to launch those good habits and by extension improve our self-discipline. When all are working properly, the new habit will become effortless, and soon all of these new actions will become a part of your own personal human make-up.

Setting Up a Good Routine

Start setting up a regular routine for yourself. This will start to give your life structure and familiarity, both are ways to put less stress on the brain. When you have structure in your life, everything begins to make more sense to you. You will begin to experience feelings of ownership and responsibility towards the things that affect you.

It also simplifies your life, eliminating the need to constantly do schedules ahead of time. You already know what you will be doing every day and when you have completed them all you have a sense of satisfaction that serves as a reward. You go to bed feeling good about your day rather than feeling stressed.

Since we are all creatures of habit, when you have a daily routine, it is much easier to incorporate those good habits into your life. When you make the decision to do these things you are becoming active participants in your life rather than just allowing habits to happen to you. It also increases efficiency, so you can get things done much quicker without having to have constant reminders that these things need to be done, which can save you lots of time and effort as you start to develop these new skills.

Finding a System That Works for You

We all have things that need to be done every day, week, or month and without a good routine, these things can easily overwhelm us. There are a lot of people who will readily tell you to follow this routine or that one, but the key to successful self-discipline is to set up a routine or a system that works best for you. Doing this may involve a little bit of creativity on your part but once you do, getting those habits under your belt will be much easier.

- Start by making a list of all your required tasks
    - This is called the gathering information stage. Consider it a complete brain dump and just jot down everything that needs to be done. You can divide the list up by daily chores, weekly, monthly, and even annually.
- Create a schedule that you feel comfortable with
    - Assess your energy level. Some people are morning people and others are night owls. Think about when you do your best work. Assign the biggest projects for the time when you are at your peak and save those lighter jobs for times when you don't need to put up so much effort.
- Leave room for some flexibility

- ❖ Don't make your schedule too tight so that you have some wiggle room in case something else comes up.
- ❖ Test it out
  - ❖ Once your routine is completed, test it out to make sure that there are no problems or challenges with following it. Make any adjustments that are needed and then do a retest to make sure it is working well for you.

It is not just important to have a good routine, but also to have one that fits well with how your body works. If you're not a morning person and you're dragging yourself out of bed every morning, then you're not going to perform at your peak. When you can optimize your time and assign tasks based on your circadian rhythm, then you're more likely to develop good habits and stick to them, which will only work to boost your self-discipline even further.

Bad Habits You Need to Avoid

Just like you want to develop good habits, it's also time to shed yourself of many of the bad habits that may be consuming your energy. One thing that will make it easier to shed those bad habits is to not just get rid of them entirely; that would leave a void, which would make you feel empty and lost. However, if you think of just trading a bad habit for a new one, the adjustment will be much simpler.

Even many of the habits listed below may seem a bit insignificant, but they are bad for you mentally, physically, emotionally and even socially. You'll find some of these will be harder than others to quit but don't let that get in the way of getting rid of them. You'll feel better, have a clearer head and find yourself much more focused and stable on the other end.

Stress Eating: Eating whenever you have a negative mood is not only dangerous to your physical health but to your emotional composition as well. Stress eating has nothing to do with your body's needs but is a replacement for emotional voids you might be feeling. By analyzing your emotional needs and addressing the true problem you're facing, your need to stress eat will eventually go away and you'll be a more emotionally balanced person as well.

Watch Your Associations: We all need socialization but when you spend too much time with those who can only see the negative in any situation you lose the value to be gained from the association. These people deplete your energy and destroy your dreams, many with the belief that they are trying to protect you. Let's face it, we are already our own worst critics and we don't need help in those areas.

Start surrounding yourself with those who will support and help you with your goals rather than tear you down.

This also applies to those who often take advantage of you. It is good to be kind and helpful to others, but if you're not getting that kind of support in return, you need to draw the line and step away from the relationship. These kinds of people can be toxic and in time will damage your spirit and hold you back from everything you are trying to do.

Smoking: Little needs to be said about the health risks of smoking. It is the leading cause of preventable death in the United States. And current research also shows the damage also extends to giving many health issues to those around you who get to inhale your second-hand smoke.

Excessive Drinking: Drinking alcohol can be fun when in a social environment, but when you drink in excess it often leads to:

- ❖ Poorer brain function: Alcohol interrupts the brain's neural pathways, making it more difficult to think clearly.
- ❖ Contributes to heart disease: It has been connected to Cardiomyopathy, arrhythmias, and other heart problems.

- Liver disease: It has been long known that excessive drinking contributes to cirrhosis, alcoholic hepatitis, and fatty liver.
- Pancreas problems: Alcohol can also lead to pancreatitis, an inflammation of the blood vessels in the pancreas, which can interfere with proper digestion.
- Cancer: It has also been connected to mouth, throat, liver, breast, and oesophageal cancers

Eating Junk Food: Junk food is a mainstay in many people's lives today. We love it because it is fast and tasty. However, but eating too much of it can alter your brain activity and can affect your behavior in a similar way to taking drugs.

Watching too Much TV: Watching TV can be very addictive. Most of us turn it on because it is a good way to unwind, but if you're not careful, it can literally take over your life, and not for the better. Start weaning yourself away from the boob tube, and replace that habit with meditation, reading, or some other productive habit that will help you to grow as a person.

Always Late: There are some people who are notoriously known for being late to everything. You know them, they are always rushing from one place to another, and seem to be behind in everything they do. Learn to be more punctual when doing things. It will help to improve your relationships, and you'll be able to relax better in your life. If this is the kind of person you are, start focusing on arriving at your destination at least 15 minutes early and you'll see positive results.

Only Seeing the Negative: When nothing seems to be going your way, it is easy to only see the negative in a given situation. It can easily become a habit to play the devil's advocate, but that doesn't inspire you to do things. Instead, it moves you to curl up in a ball and hibernate. No matter how bad a situation is, work to identify 3 positive things in every situation and by the time you've made it a habit, you'll have a much more positive outlook on life.

This is not to say that all of these habits are bad. We all have bad moods from time to time and we all get discouraged, worried, and experience a host of negative emotions. However, when they become a major part of our lives, they will definitely interfere with our growth and we'll find ourselves never progressing in the things we want to do. By replacing those bad habits with more positive good ones, we remove one more element that may be interfering with our ability to strengthen our self-defense.

Chapter 6

GETTING OUT OF YOUR COMFORT ZONE

All of us have an internal desire to step out of our comfort zone at some point. We see other people doing exciting things and we internally want to be a part of something new and thrilling. But even though that desire exists, something gets in our way, and we find ourselves literally paralyzed in the cocoon of comfort we've made.

There is a scientific explanation as to why it is so difficult to break free from our comfort zone and with a little understanding of what it really is, you can make a few simple adjustments that will allow you to do so.

What is Your Comfort Zone?

Your comfort zone is a behavioral dynamic where your routines and habits all fit together nicely. It is the safe place you go to where there is a minimal risk (or at least risk that is manageable) and by extension less stress. When you are in your comfort zone, you are mentally secure, content, with low anxiety and stress.

While staying in your comfort zone lowers your level of stress and it gives you a 'safe haven' from the unknown world around you, it has its own limitations. As long as you remain in that low stress environment, you cannot progress or grow. This is because in order to improve at anything our stress levels have to be slightly higher than what we experience when we are comfortable. If we stay in that place for too long, we cannot progress.

It is true, your comfort zone can be a good thing. It is a safe place where you can go mentally and emotionally. Leaving it means taking on a whole new set of risks and venturing into uncharted territory, which could turn out to be either positive or it could be negative. But there is a good reason to try to break out of that safe spot and seek out new things.

What You're Missing Out On

Pushing to the point where you can grow is the only place where you can improve your performance in anything you do. It enhances your productivity and gives you a lot more skills you'll be able to rely on. Think about some of these benefits when it comes to stepping out of your comfort zone.

- **Increased Productivity:** No one enjoys the pressure that comes with deadlines and expectations placed on us. If we stay in our comfort zone, we do the minimum required for us to get by. Without the internal drive to do more and learn new things, we fall into a pattern of appearing busy but leaving our minds free to wander wherever they may go. But, if you push beyond that flatline, you'll be able to find smarter ways to work and get more done at the same time.
- **Adapt Better to Changes:** Regularly stepping out of our comfort zone, pushing the boundaries teaches you how to adapt to changes better. If you regularly push the limits, taking risks in a controlled manner, challenging yourself in various new environments, you learn to adjust to things that make you uncomfortable. As a result, you widen your comfort zone allowing you to incorporate more things in your daily life.
- **It'll Get Easier:** After you've pushed the boundaries a few times, it won't be so frightening or difficult to do. Regularly opening up to new ideas can teach us new things, allow us to see the world in a whole new way, and inspire us to expand even more. Each time we do, we learn to view the world

in a different light, and we are more motivated to expend our energy in wildly rewarding ways.

There are many benefits to widening our comfort zone that can linger far longer than the initial fear you might have experienced in the beginning. The advancements you'll gain through new skills, and experiences will far outweigh the negatives you might be worrying about.

How it Relates to Fear

It is easy to understand the fear that is related to our comfort zone. Few people would doubt that it is at the core of everyone's hesitation. If you were to imagine a bullseye positioned right in front of you, that inner circle, would represent your comfort zone. But another word you could label that circle with is 'fear.' Once we come to understand how much fear is controlling our unwillingness to take those brave steps outward, we begin to see our comfort as a place to hide from the scary things in life.

It is perfectly normal to fear dangerous things. When we walk along the edge of a cliff, we experience fear because we don't want to fall. When we drive too fast in a car, we become fearful because we know the consequences of a crash, and a child is fearful when he sees his mother leave him at school for the first time. Under most circumstances, fear is a perfectly normal reaction to the dangers of life. But look at your bullseye again. Just outside the bullseye, you have labeled as your comfort/fear zone is another circle. Call this your learning circle. If you remain in your fear spot, you will never reach the point of learning anything new, so you will have to overcome that in order to grow.

F.E.A.R

Understanding what fear really is can help us to break this habit. Fear can be broken down into a simple phrase:

False

Expectations

Appearing

Real

Think about all the things you are afraid of. Whether it is speaking in public or traveling to a new country. Most of it comes from worry about what you think will happen. It's all in the future, and your mind is playing various scenarios about the possibilities. You are allowing your mind to create false expectations.

Let's take speaking in public, for example. Most people have that fear of speaking out in public. What goes through your mind when you have to speak in front of people. You automatically think, 'they won't like me,' 'I'll forget what I have to say,' 'I'll mess up' or 'They'll boo me.' We all think like that or we think of something similar. But, in reality, those kinds of things never really happen. Our minds have just convinced us that we are not worthy of respect, appreciation, reward, or whatever and as a result, our minds will create the worst possible scenario in any given situation.

Since we cannot predict the future, and the odds of those things happening are very limited, our minds have created these false expectations and delivered to them to us as fact, therefore paralyzing us to the point that we are not able to act. This doesn't mean that you have to push the boundaries all the time. There is nothing wrong with being comfortable, but if we get too comfortable and never challenge ourselves, our comfort zone will become stagnant and our world and the things in it will shrink. We need to push the limits sometimes in order to grow.

Fear and Your Own Distractions

One way we avoid venturing off into growth territory is through distractions. This is the time when we turn on the TV or decide to call that long lost friend we haven't talked to in ages. Distractions like these can be a healthy outlet when under stress but they can also be a tool of avoidance that we have to overcome.

They can have a real powerful influence over us. All of us have a limited attention span and when we divert our attention to something else we are not able to fully focus our minds on anything else. But in reality, when this happens, it is not the distraction that is at the root of your problem. It is your internal desire to be distracted that needs to be fixed. The distraction is merely a by-product of your fears.

We deliberately seek distractions because of our fears and this is what keeps us from stepping out of our comfort zone. You, therefore, need to develop strategies to train your mental powers to be brave and to push past all of those doubts, insecurities, and fears.

Training Your Mind to be Brave

You can step out of your comfort zone and test the waters on the outside. By following some basic strategies, you can start small and build up on your successes until you reach the point where you are brave enough to venture boldly into new territory. You might want to play it close to the vest at first, but as you progress, you'll find that stretching the limits can literally bring out the best in you.

- ❖ Do routine things a little differently: This initial step allows you to stay within your comfort zone without experiencing something completely new. If you drive to work every day, rather than take the same route, try a new one. Chances are you are very familiar with the different roads in your community, so you won't be driving in unfamiliar territory. You're only changing the time you are on that particular road. This puts familiar things in a different light. After you have successfully changed some of your routine habits this way, you'll start to feel a little more confidence in your ability to do something different.

- ❖ Slow down: When we are in our comfort zone, we live mostly on automatic pilot and we can whisk through tasks without even realizing we're doing them. Learning to slow down on unfamiliar tasks can quickly make you uncomfortable. Take the time to do things at a slower pace, taking note of your actions. As you do, observe your task as an outsider, and then try to intervene and come up with different more efficient ways to improve them. Mentally defend your reasons for doing things the way you do. This might be enough to give you a little nudge to make some changes in your life.

- ❖ Make a snap decision: Every now and then, make a decision without thinking. When we have to step out of our comfort zone, we tend to overthink things and often dedicate a lot of time to finding reasons not to do something. It doesn't have to be a major decision, so start by considering something small. If you eat at the same place every day, consider trying a new place. If you eat the same foods all the time, try something new. It will give your learning curve a kickstart and teach you that you are fully capable of trusting your inner judgment.
- ❖ Make small, incremental steps: In the beginning, it will be difficult to make even the smallest step, but if you can muster up the courage to take those tiny little baby steps, you will still get the same benefits as you would the bigger ones. Whether you jump into the water with both feet or you start by sticking one toe in, you're going to get wet just the same. Don't push too far, and you might be surprised at where you end up, one little tiny baby step at a time.

The most difficult part about this is taking that first step. If you keep these basic truths in mind, you will be able to succeed in this journey.

1. Take an honest look at your life. The first step out of familiar territory requires you to take a good and honest look at who you are. You need to be able to identify your starting point. Analyse yourself and take note of the patterns, thoughts, and desires you have. Write them on physical paper, that makes them feel a lot more real.
2. Start with changes that pose no threat. They are simple and safe even if they are unfamiliar.
3. Allow yourself to fail sometimes. You'll learn that you won't die or be harmed from failure. You'll live to try another day. When you literally fall, most often it is not the pain that causes you distress, but rather it is the unfamiliarity with the sensation. Learning how to fail will allow you to get familiar with new sensations and when you survive them, they won't be so scary anymore.

There are many ways you can discover to break out of your comfort zone. Whether you want to travel the globe or just get rid of your shyness, you already know you're missing out. Trying new things can be a little scary at times but doing so will help you to push your body and mind forward into areas where you never thought you would go. And you know what you gain from doing new things? More self-confidence, which naturally leads to better self-discipline.

Chapter 7

Managing Your Environment

It is important to have control of your environment. We don't realize just how our environment can influence our behavior. Most people believe that we do the things we do because it is part of who we are, but in reality, many times we behave a certain way because of where we are. When studies have been performed among participants from different countries in Europe, results showed that the answer to the same question will vary widely with more people answering the way those in their same communities our countries answer.

For example, a global study was conducted and participants were asked one simple question. "Would you like to be an organ donor?" The answered revealed some surprising results. Those in the countries of Denmark, the Netherlands, the United Kingdom, and Germany had a far larger percentage of negative answers than those of other European countries. You might assume that the results were skewed based on religious or cultural differences, but it was not the case. Since all of the countries were European there wasn't much difference between their religions and cultures.

On closer inspection, we learn that regardless of the way the question is presented, the majority of participants will choose the answer that allows them the least risk of changing a regular habit. This is a tendency referred to as the 'default effect'. While that particular study was conducted in Europe, the same kinds of results showed in in other studies around the globe.

This teaches us that we have an inborn tendency to stay with what we are familiar with. Whether it's where or when we turn on the TV or when we sleep at night, we always default to what is familiar. So, with that thought in mind, it is important to exercise some control over our environment or we will quickly find that our environment will begin to control us.

How your environment plays a role

We all have a default that we refer back to in any given situation. When it comes to breakfast, we usually try to eat the same thing every day. Most people can't get moving without their morning cup of coffee, and how many of us actually would rather watch TV than read a book?

It is time for you to determine what your default environment look like. If it is working towards supporting you in your quest to build self-discipline then good, but if it is going against everything you're trying to do, then you need to think of ways to change it. You want an environment that will encourage you to step out of your comfort zone, learn and try new things, and be instrumental in helping you grow as a person. It should support those behaviors that you want to build on and discourage those that are holding you back.

Setting up the Proper Environment

When you change your environment you literally are changing the kind of results you get. If your surroundings make it easy to make the changes you want in your life and hard to continue with the unwanted behaviors building self-discipline. However, if your environment does the opposite, you will struggle at every turn. Ideally, you want an environment that encourages good habits and makes them your default.

This is not as easy as it sounds. In the beginning, you may find yourself falling back on those past default behaviors when under stress. They are like a knee-jerk reaction that you can't help. But, if you set up the right environment from the start, those times when you revert to old habits will become fewer and fewer.

Objects: We should also think of how objects around us can affect us. You may not think this is true, reasoning that it is just an inanimate object. But think about how you feel when you're visiting a nice national park far away from the city, breathing in the clean fresh air, and taking in the beautiful sights of nature.

Now imagine that you are in a busy metropolis. Cars honking, lights flashing, and noise everywhere. Fast food papers and cups litter the street, and there is disorder all around you. Now, compare the difference in how you feel. In the first one, you probably feel relaxed and even refreshed, but in the second one, you are likely beginning to feel a little stressed.

We may feel that our unique and distinctive personality anchors us, we subconsciously respond to contextual cues in our environment. While we are all different (some of us may enjoy the busy city and thrive on it, and others may hate the great outdoors) take the time to look at your environment and analyze whether it is supporting you in your change or not. If not, think of ways you can adjust your surroundings in order to give you a sense of being grounded in a positive new future.

People: It has been proven over and over again that people often conform to what the masses do. Even if you know something is wrong, if everyone around you is going in another direction, you are faced with a choice. Do you follow the crowd or do you go it alone? The correct answer is obvious, but the results bear witness to the fact that most people will just conform to what everyone else is doing.

When everyone seems convinced that one way is right, you begin to question your own personal judgment. You assume that something must be wrong because everyone else can't possibly be wrong.

This is because humans are social creatures and we have a powerful internal need to be accepted. This is a natural drive to adapt to the people around us and can be very practical, but it can also be very harmful. We often let society dictate what is right or wrong in our environment, so we end up hanging out with people who are not supportive, pessimistic, or just plain old lazy. As a result, when you decide to do something out of the norm, the collective will do their best to get you to conform to what they consider the norm and hold you back. This is why surrounding yourself with positive people who are enthusiastic and encouraging will help you to develop your new skills much, much faster.

This type of group psychology is contagious. There is power in your social environment so be selective about those you want to include in your inner circle. Whether you realize it or not, people are like infections looking for someone vulnerable enough to influence. If you want to protect your dreams, emotions, beliefs, and ideals you can't ignore the kind of influence that other people will have on you.

Conditions: Designing the right conditions for your success is only going to support your self-discipline. In creating your own unique environment, you will have to exercise your will power in order to get the results you're looking for.

Still, we can't just will the conditions of our environment to change, we must make some practical decisions in order for things to happen. For example, you may know of an excellent restaurant to go to where they serve incredibly delicious meals, but you wouldn't go there if you're looking to lose weight. If you're looking for a delicious dish to enjoy, you'll find a more practical choice to make.

This will require testing out different conditions until you find the one that best suits the goals you are trying to meet. Remember, you only have so much willpower to go around and you don't want to deplete it by spending all of your time in environmental conditions that will work against you. Your goal is to create an environment that won't distract you or put roadblocks in your way.

Ideally, your environmental conditions should have the following elements in order to foster the kind of growth you are pursuing.

- ❖ It should limit the number of distractions you have to deal with. If your environment is full of distractions, you will find it difficult to maintain your concentration when you need to. We are naturally inclined to take the path of least resistance regardless of the situation. Why not make that path one that leads you to your goal? So, if you're living in a cluttered environment, take the time to clean it up. This promotes a clear mind, which is much easier to maintain discipline.
- ❖ Make it an effort to eliminate those more desirable temptations: We may not be able to rid ourselves of all distractions, especially if we are inclined to share them with other people. However, you could make sure that temptation is placed in an area where it will take some effort to use them. If you have to put up too much effort to walk across the room to get something to eat, then you are likely to put it off for

a longer period of time than if you had delicious food choices right at your fingertips.

❖ Control your dopamine: Dopamine is a pleasure hormone that is released in the body any time we are enjoying ourselves. When our brain secretes dopamine, we feel good. It is the sensation we get when we are involved in sex, drugs, or listening to music. Since we like feeling good, we opt to make those things our priorities. In some cases, if you're developing a good habit this can work to your benefit, but, more often than not, it can pose a real danger to your growth. It is possible to develop a dopamine addiction, which can kill all your attempts at improving your self-discipline. This is another reason why removing distractions is so important, dopamine can be released when we engage in pleasurable activities, but it can also be released by the anticipation of those same activities. So, if the distractions are moved far away from you, you are less likely to be tempted. Remember the old saying, 'out of sight, out of mind.' Those distractions like social media pages, emails, and your favorite TV shows have historically been known to have a huge impact on viewers.

❖ Make sure your default position is positive: Your environment should make it easy to fall back on your positive default positions. By doing this, you increase your chances of making that into a real habit. By optimizing your default behaviour, the majority of your effort will be conducive to self-discipline. If it is too easy to turn on your computer or the remote, you'll make those things your priority. If you have a problem with spending too much time on social media, consider making it harder to access. Delete your favorite apps from your device or at least log out after each use. That will require more effort for you to use them the next time you want to use them.

The whole goal of managing your environment is to conserve your energy and willpower so you can dedicate them to more worthwhile endeavors.

Chapter 8

Difference Between Being Productive and Being Busy

We live in an intense world where everything moves at the speed of light. People have an unusual drive to stay connected to everything around them and as a result, they often give the appearance of being busy all the time. Part of the reason for this is because to a certain extent, we want the respect of others. If we look busy then we must be important, successful, or happy. No doubt about it, busy people generally are looking for an ego boost.

When we say we are busy, it is often an avoidance tactic. We are building up an excuse for doing something we simply do not want to do. Granted, there are plenty of times when we are truly busy and we cannot carve out another second, but most will admit, that the word 'busy' has become a catchall phrase for 'I don't want to do it.'

For anyone who sincerely wants to change the dynamics so they can become more productive, start to find the time to incorporate new things into your schedule.

Think about when you really want to do something, how easy it is to move things around so you can squeeze it in. To improve your self-discipline, you will need to start making room for other things in your life. The more you have to manage, the easier it is to keep yourself on target.

This doesn't mean that you are never truly busy. You may be spending your entire days putting out one fire or another. But that doesn't mean that you are being productive. A common word spread among busy people is "multi-tasking.' People often say that they are multitasking. They are being productive by working on more than one thing at a time. However, according to one study conducted by Stanford Professor Clifford Nass, those who were chronic multitaskers were consistently outperformed by those who were not. The results of the study showed that even when given tasks that allowed them to focus on only one thing at a time, multitaskers were still not using their brains effectively. These results give impressive evidence that a chaotic and disorganized mind even though it seems busy is not the best approach to situations. For that reason, you need to self-analyze yourself to determine if you are truly being productive in your tasks or you're just busy.

❖ Check your to do list: If your to do list is very long, chances are you're not being very productive. When you are truly productive, you can afford to be more selective about the amount of work you accept, and you are capable of creating a strategic plan to accomplish your tasks as soon as possible.

- ❖ Are you prioritizing your work: When you are busy, you take whichever action comes first in no specific order. When you learn how to prioritize tasks, you decide which ones are more important or more time-consuming and you tackle those first. Handling those when your energy level is higher will be an extra assurance that you will get them done within a reasonable amount of time.
- ❖ Record your progress: When you are busy, you give the appearance of something being done. You equate action or movement with progress. You put a lot of things into a single day so by the end of the day something must be completed, right? But often when you have this long list of tasks that you're trying to do at one time, you may only accomplish one or two a day but have twenty more that are only partially done. When you are productive, you avoid taking on random tasks and take the most strategic approach to accomplishments.

While you may have thought being busy was a good thing, and sometimes it is, being productive is a much more valuable skill to have. Anyone can make the switch at any time to a more productive lifestyle. When you tackle things first by importance and in a specific order, you'll find that you're spending less energy and less time to get things done. Your self-discipline will improve along with your efficiency.

Know What Needs to Get Done

To become more productive, you need to prioritize your tasks. This will provide more order in your life and give you focus. When you prioritize, important things are always accomplished first. But, how do you choose what is important and must get done and what can be put off for later. More importantly, what do you do when everything on your to do list is important but you're working with limited time.

As you look at your list of things to do, take the time to ask these very important questions:

1. Why is it important?

We all have a tendency to procrastinate from time to time, even with important things but we may not realize it. We may subconsciously dedicate a great deal of time to smaller and less important tasks because the bigger ones are just too big. In reality, whether we're doing things for your job or you're trying to get housework done, you know what you should be working on and what is important and what is not. If you don't, asking the question can reveal a lot about how to prioritize each task. When you choose an important task to work on, you know that part of your job will be done, which should give you some level of satisfaction. It also can be self-rewarding to know that you're making a difference in how your day is going to go.

2. Choose your most important task to do first

When you start your day, choose your most important task to do first. While it may be okay to do it at any time of the day, there are definite advantages to getting it done first. At the beginning of each day, start by writing your to do list and then prioritizing them with the most important on top and then each successive task should be listed by importance. This is an excellent way to get your job done and channel your energy at the same time. It will automatically improve your focus. You could also do this the night before. That way, you are already focused when you wake up the next morning because you know exactly what you're going to do for that day.

3. What Qualifies as an Important Task

When you have a lot of things to do, it can be difficult to determine what is most important. It may mean that you have to take the time to analyse your list and what is required of each task. If your job is to create marketing plans, chances are working on the plan itself will weigh more heavily than answering social media posts or checking emails. In most cases, the answer will be obvious but in other cases, it may take a little trial and error before you can effectively prioritize your list. To find out the most important task for you, consider what is most urgent, or what will make the biggest impact.

4. When there are more than one extremely important tasks

Sometimes you will have more than one urgent task that needs to get done. You need to focus on only one at a time. If they are of equal importance, then it won't matter which one you do first, as long as you get started. If you're still unsure about which one to start with, try picking the one that you are most excited about.

5. Tackling Smaller Tasks

No matter how long your list is, always focus on your most important tasks first. Then once they are done, turn your attention to those less urgent needs. You may not complete them all in a single day so if you finish without having them all done, it's okay because you have your most important things already completed, you can finish your day satisfied that you have been productive.

Identify Your Avoidance Tendencies

We all have our own set of avoidance tendencies that we use when we don't want to do something. We may not even realize we're using them, but they seem to automatically spring up anytime we want to get out of an uncomfortable situation. Because this behavior comes up automatically, we can assume it is a well engrained habit that we've come to rely on. Likely it developed because of the temporary relief we feel when we are able to escape from whatever it is we didn't want to do.

Avoidant patterns if not addressed can lead to not only the inability to grow but also will eventually lead to excessive anxiety in many situations. As a result, you need to identify those patterns in your own life and deal with them so that you won't automatically revert to them when certain situations arise. There are many different types of avoidance tendencies, but they generally relate to internal fears you might have. Some examples might be:

- ❖ Avoiding tasks that require interpersonal connections
- ❖ Avoiding associating with others for fear of not being liked
- ❖ Avoiding personal or intimate relationships
- ❖ Fear of being criticized in social settings
- ❖ Fear of new social environments
- ❖ Not taking reasonable risks
- ❖ Avoiding participating in situations you perceive may be embarrassing

These are just some of the possibilities involved in avoidance tendencies. They can come in a wide variety of forms, but when faced with a situation where you are perfectly qualified to do but are afraid of a negative consequence, assume that the excuse you give is an avoidance tendency. If you're not sure you're using these tendencies, then stop and ask yourself why you're not willing to do a certain activity. If it is an avoidance tendency, then it will be directly related to a fear of some sort.

To identify your avoidance tendencies, you first need to have some level of understanding of how you've developed the patterns. Most of the time these are not recognizable because they started in childhood. Fears usually develop because of a traumatic experience you've had in your past. Or they may have developed the habit from the modeling of a specific parent who used the same tactics. It is much harder for one to learn to adjust if this kind of behavior is all they know. There are at least nine different signs that you are using avoidance tendencies to get out of things you're uncomfortable doing.

- ❖ You don't do things that may trigger painful memories
- ❖ You live your life under the radar
- ❖ You avoid facing reality and officially confirming your thinking
- ❖ You do whatever is necessary to keep people from being angry at you
- ❖ You stop working whenever an uncomfortable thought comes up
- ❖ You avoid any situation where you might feel uncomfortable
- ❖ You won't start anything unless you know how to finish it
- ❖ You avoid certain physical sensations
- ❖ You avoid any situation where you may not be as good as someone else

These kinds of tendencies are bad habits that can cause you to procrastinate or never start your job at all. Once you are able to recognize that these tendencies have become a habit, you can then take the necessary steps to change them so that you can move on. By eliminating these practices from your life, you free up another obstacle that could interfere with improving your self-discipline.

Many people who rely heavily on avoidance tendencies grew up in households where there was a lot of conflict and the parents either avoided direct conflict or it was poorly managed. As a result, they never learned how to face uncomfortable situations head on. Being able to understand how you have developed these tendencies is key to mastering your ability to overcome them.

Chapter 9

THE 80/20 RULE

Whether you are working on building up your self-esteem or not, knowing the 80/20 rule can be of benefit to everyone. The name sounds a bit like a statistic, but it runs much deeper than the concept of some abstract number applied to a given scenario. The concept has its roots deep into economics but can be understood and applied by those who are not economic geniuses. Its basic principle is:

It was named after the Italian economist Vilfredo Pareto, who observed that 80% of income in Italy was received by 20% of the population. The assumption is that most of the results in any given situation can be determined by a small number of causes.

While this concept was originally written with economics in view, it soon became evident that it applied to all aspects of life. So, let's try to break down the 80/20 rule and how it applies to building up your self-discipline.

The Pareto Principle

To put it simply. It means that 80% of your results come from 20% of what you put into it. This fact seems to consistently hold true in a wide variety of situations. In reality, the numbers don't really matter, the general idea is that a lot more results go to only a few people.

If you haven't heard this rule before, chances are you would think the numbers are a bit skewed but take the time to look at all the activities you do each day. Then try to determine how much of the work you're putting out is giving you the results you need. For most people, the evidence is clear – only a handful of activities you dedicate yourself to produce the income and things you need to live.

For example, look at the distribution of wealth and resources we need every day. A very small percentage of the global population has control over the world's resources. The money that businesses generate is usually earned by 20% of the workforce. Only about 20% of the customers for a business generate about 80% of its total revenue. While this number may not be consistent, it does make it clear that there is a wide disparity where the majority of those involved are served by the few.

On a smaller scale, take a closer look at your own life. Where are you putting the most energy? You may be making a lot of phone calls every day, but the benefits of those calls only come from a few people. Your Facebook page probably has lots of friends, but how many of those friends are those you can rely on. You likely only spend quality time with a few of them even though you may have several hundred.

On a personal level, look at your schedule. How much time are you spending on your passion projects that are not yielding financial results? While they can be fun and exciting to do, you know they won't pay the bills. We may find a great deal of our time is spent on these activities, which is another way of procrastinating so that we are not efficient in our work.

Living an 80/20 Life

Once you start analyzing this common thread in your life, you begin to see these ratios everywhere. The key to turning this around is to try to push out that 80% of the effort you're giving and work only on the 20% that will produce the best results. It's not about working harder but working smarter.

Therefore, you want to focus on those activities that will yield the best results for you. This doesn't just have to apply in a monetary way, but it can also apply on a personal level. So, whether your goal is to become an artist who is looking to be discovered, or you want to bring your family closer together, it is important to take the time and analyze the activities you are involved in and trim the fat. Focus most of your energy on those things that produce results and leave the rest for another time.

How Does This Apply to Self-Discipline

When you have good self-discipline, you are already in the 20% of skills that produce the 80% results. It is the one ingredient that is necessary for all sorts of interactions including collaboration. Self-discipline is only useful if you apply it to the 20% of activities that will yield results. For example, you can apply your self-discipline to not playing video games, which could free up some time for you but may not otherwise yield any productive results. You can discipline yourself to not watch TV, but then again, while there are some benefits to that exercise, if it's not producing the kind of results you need, then you're spinning your wheels.

However, if you are applying your self-discipline to developing good and productive habits, these are things that will stick with you until they become second nature. Your new habits become a bunch of little rules that will guide you to those 20% of activities that will yield the best results. In the end, you can conclude that 80% of the results you gain from building your self-discipline will come from applying 20% of your effort to developing new and productive habits.

If we all do this, we will be more inclined to stick with building our self-discipline as we will come to realize that it is like a golden ticket to the kind of results we're seeking. You will become a self-starter rather than having someone tell you where to go. You will learn discretion but at the same time, learn how to walk off the beaten path. In the end, you will have a lot more freedom than you might otherwise have.

Conclusion

Thanks for making it through to the end of Self-Discipline: Mastery of the Mind, let's hope it was informative and able to provide you with all of the tools you need to achieve your goals whatever it may be.

Your self-discipline is like a muscle that you need to exercise every day. Even after you have mastered this skill, you will still need to exercise this muscle or it will start to become flabby again. If you fall out of practice, all the skills you've learned will evaporate and you will have to start all over again.

Use the information you learned here but never assume that you have completed your journey. Those who have strong skills in this area never cut corners, take breaks, or make excuses. You need to be true to yourself and resist the impulse to think you've got it made. Keep working at it until it becomes a habit, and then keep working at it some more.

You'll know when you are using your self-discipline in the right way; you'll know when to say 'no' to things that will take you away from what's important. You won't have to think about it or weigh your options, your brain will have been trained like a fine-tuned musical instrument to play when the right cue is recognized.

This doesn't mean that you won't have any distractions and that you won't be tempted. Those are actual parts of life and they will never go away. What will go away after you've mastered these techniques is their effect on you.

Together we have discussed many things. By now you will understand:

- What is self-discipline
- How to take your first steps
- Why you need to have a purpose
- How to identify your self-discipline problems
- How to replace bad habits with new ones
- The power fear has over you
- How to get out of your comfort zone
- And more.

You can only go up from here. We have not been able to learn every little aspect of self-discipline but are confident that you can take it from here. There is no end to the education you can learn and how it will make you grow. It is our hope that once you've put yourself in the right frame of mind, good physical condition, and gotten rid of your fears that you will be ready to apply your self-discipline in every aspect of your life.

Self-Compassion

Learn To Love Yourself The Way You Are

Kristin Carmichael   &   Kyle Neff

Chapter 1

WHAT IS SELF-COMPASSION

In order to understand the word self-compassion it would be helpful to comprehend what the word compassion means. Literally compassion means to feel sympathy or to suffer with.

It is a general view that the suffering of others, motivates us to feel compassion for them. Consider a situation, where you are on your way to your office and you see a homeless person begging, you might actually stop to consider his adverse situation. Your heart might feel like it has a connection with that of the beggar's. You do not feel like ignoring him and you are urged by your inner self to help him in some way. That feeling is accurately described as compassion. It is clear from this example that compassion entails feelings of care, kindness and understanding for the people in pain.

Self-compassion has exactly the same attributes, the only difference is that the compassion is turned inwards. Self-compassion is not just an individual feeling, it has three important dimensions; self-kindness, mindfulness and common humanity.

Self-kindness

Self-compassion demands us to be understanding and warm to ourselves in sufferings and failure instead of criticizing oneself. One should recognize that experiencing the difficulties of life and being imperfect is inevitable, so we nurture and soothe ourselves when confronting pain instead of getting angry when we fall short of our aims. We should acknowledge our shortcoming and the fact that we cannot always achieve what we want. Otherwise if we turn our mind away from this reality and deny it, the result is the suffering in the form of frustration, stress and self-criticism. If this reality is acknowledged we are able to generate emotions of care and kindness that can help us cope with the problem.

Mindfulness

Mindfulness is a receptive and nonjudgmental state of mind in which feelings and thoughts are observed as they may be, without denying them. The response to the negative thoughts about oneself is either agonizing over them or ignoring them.

When confronted by adversities we often try to solve the problem without recognizing the dire need to calm and comfort ourselves for the adversities we are facing. The mental space that is provided by taking a mindful approach to our tough feelings allows us to have greater emotional equanimity, perspective and clarity

Common Humanity:

The biggest problem of self-judgment is that it makes us feel alone and isolated. When we come to know something about ourselves that we do not like, we see everyone else as perfect and view ourselves as inadequate. Focusing on our shortcomings renders us shortsighted and we cannot see anything apart from our own so-called "worthless" self. We also may feel abnormal. When something is wrong, we are affected by it and other people just seem to handle it better. In such situations self-compassion puts things in order and helps us to recognize the fact that other people also feel inadequate at different stages of their lives. We get to know that failures are an experience that everyone shares. This thought greatly comforts us in adversities.

At this point it is quite necessary to know which acts are not to be mistaken with self-compassion. People often confuse self-compassion with self-pity, self-indulgence and self-esteem.

Often people are reluctant to do self-compassion because they mistake it with self-pity. Self-pity is quite different from self-compassion. If someone feels self-pity they would surely become immersed in their own adversities and problems and tend to forget that other people might also have the same problems. They would feel as if they were the one out of all the others who had problems. Self-pity is characterized by the ego-centric feelings of isolation and exaggerates the magnitude of personal distress. On the other hand in self-compassion people acknowledge that they are not the only one in harsh situations and this thought greatly comforts them.

An even greater stigma on self-compassion is that people think of it to be some kind of self-indulgence. Some people believe that self-criticism is quite necessary to motivate oneself, otherwise if they are too self-compassionate they will just sit around wasting their time, is there any truth to this? It can be explained by the example of how parents motivate young ones. When the parents care about their children and desire their well-being, do they indulge by allowing them to do whatever they want? No. They will make sure that their children eat well, brush their teeth, go to school regularly, finish their home work and sleep early because it is necessary for them to be healthy and live a good life. Their children will surely be motivated to reach their goals in life and can count on their parents' support even if they fail.

Now let's consider the situation where the parents ruthlessly criticize their children when they mess up and tell them that they are failures, how is it going to make the children feel? Motivated, inspired, ready to achieve their goals? Certainly not. Constant criticism can make us feel depressed and worthless, not exactly the keep-moving-on mindset. Isn't it the same manner in which we treat ourselves? And somehow are led to believe that self-criticism is an effective motivator than self-compassion. That's the reason why self-criticism is often linked with self-handicapping and underachievement.

Distinguishing self-compassion from self-esteem is also important. Self-esteem is the extent to which we tend to evaluate ourselves positively. It shows our liking for ourselves and is based on comparison with others. In popular cultures, having high self-esteem as compared to others means to think of oneself to be special and above other average people. On the other hand, self-compassion is not characterized by positive evaluation or judgment. It focuses on interconnections instead of separateness, moreover it provides emotional stability.

Chapter 2

WHY YOU MIGHT LACK SELF-COMPASSION

Now that we see and know ourselves, or more importantly, have reached a higher degree of awareness towards ourselves, we are now capable of truly loving who we are. Having found out about our strengths and most especially our weaknesses, we are now capable of focusing on the things that we need to nurture ourselves. We know now which parts of us we need to heal. Some of us might equate self-love with pride, but these two are things from very different worlds. Pride is tolerating one's negative aspects thinking it is self-love to preserve one's ego but it is not. Self-love is when you decide to nurture yourself and desire growth for yourself because you want to see yourself become better, no matter how uncomfortable that may be. It takes a lot of self-love for one to be able to do that. But believe me, if you haven't done so for yourself yet, self-love is perhaps the most beautiful thing you can ever give to yourself in this world. For it only means you give yourself absolute independence from the rest of the world. Loving yourself gives you the power not to need anyone's validation.

For one thing that everyone needs to learn, is that ultimately, our constant companion, is but ourselves. No one else, not even our closest loved one, is going to stay with us all the time except ourselves. Hence, we must learn to love our own companionship. For that to happen, we must love ourselves completely that we treat ourselves with utmost care. How many of us here love themselves so much they wouldn't dare hurt one's self? Not just physically, but mentally and spiritually. A lot of us here, are mean even to ourselves, maybe not intentionally but we do so all the same. How can that be? Well, whenever we tell ourselves negative things that in itself is already a form of self-abuse. Whenever we look at ourselves in the mirror and conclude to ourselves for example that we are unattractive, isn't it that we feel bad for ourselves? And ironically, we felt bad because we made ourselves feel bad in the first place by saying something negative about ourselves. If by any chance, you are that kind of person, isn't it that by doing so you become a lousy companion to yourself? What's worse is that whenever someone else tells you negative things about yourself, you would believe them, not necessarily because it's true, but more so because you believe in it yourself.

Hence, self-love is practically self-positive reaffirmation. We must be able to love our selves so much that we are capable of self-compassion or self-empathy.

Being compassionate to ourselves to the point that we are never going to say or think anything negative about ourselves. To be able to treat ourselves with so much respect that we are incapable of doing anything remotely disrespectful to our own beings. In other words, we ourselves are also our own best friends. Whenever we feel down or discouraged, us ourselves are the ones who lifts ourselves up and encourages ourselves to become more motivated. We ourselves are the ones who greatly strive to be able to get for ourselves the things we want and desire most. Having lots of self-love then enables us to become mentally, emotionally, and spiritually independent. In other words, we strive to become what we want and need the most. Doing so, becoming aware of the things that we want and need, physically, mentally, emotionally, and spiritually, we also then move towards the things that benefit us the most. Suddenly, we find ourselves giving less and less time doing things that doesn't help us grow. In turn, surrounding us with lots of self-love and attention, we feel a higher amount of satisfaction in our lives. As opposed to asking for all these things from other people. Most certainly they are going to fail us from time to time. Hence, it is of great convenience that we can rely on ourselves all the time.

Not that we are going to be discouraged from entrusting ourselves to other people. Paradoxically, becoming independent of other people's love is what allows us to unconditionally love other people, and more so, it is what makes us appreciate their love even more, knowing that we didn't even need it in the first place. Now, this level of self-love that I am talking about takes a lot of time to develop. Before we can achieve it, we need incredible amounts of self-awareness. Being able to figure ourselves out completely that we know everything that we need in all aspects of our lives. And as we mentioned, this level of self-love makes us capable of unconditionally loving other people. For this self-love becomes the standard to which we love other people. For that of course is the love that we know best, the love that we give ourselves. A good question would be, what is the best possible way that we may be able to create more self-love? How is that going to manifest?

For us to know just that, what we need is self-compassion. When we are self-compassionate, then we are able to think about what's best for us. We become more aware of the things that we want and need the most and so we consciously work towards giving ourselves exactly those things. Now, of course this will depend on the personality of the person, the things that they want and need. But, what we have come to understand, is the fact that we want and need the most, is peace. For whatever situation we are in in life that is the thing that we always look for. Some might say, it is happiness, but the thing is, we can't have happiness if we do not have peace. For peace is basically the foundation for all the positive emotions or practically all the emotions that we have, without it is impossible for us to feel anything good.

In relation to all of this, overall, we become more sensitive towards ourselves giving us the ability to have more empathy. And by practicing self-empathy we are then also honed to become more thoughtful and compassionate towards others. As the very old yet always completely relevant saying goes, "Do unto others what you would want others to do unto you".

Chapter 3

Mindful Self-Compassion

Mindfulness helps you build self-love. Before we delve into how mindfulness helps you build self-love, let us understand mindfulness.

Mindfulness is the act of being present in every moment, concentrating on what you are doing at any point in time, and refusing to dwell on past mistakes and future worries.

How Mindfulness Helps You Build Self-Love

When you engage in mindful practices such as mindful breathing, meditation, yoga, etc., you simply focus your mind on the things you have been overlooking all your life. Mindfulness makes you more grateful for the things and abilities you have.

Mindfulness also enables you to take note of things that add value to your life; things you have always considered insignificant such as your ability to talk people into changing certain habits, your ability to make people smile amidst worries, your ability to come up with solutions to difficult puzzles, etc.

Mindfulness also helps you notice all the things you have going for you and enables you to love and respect whom you are.

How can you practice mindfulness to develop self-respect and improve self-love? Here are some ideas to guide you:

1: Know what you think, feel, and want most times

Mindful people keep track of their most dominant thoughts, feelings, and desires. When you become more mindful of your thoughts and feelings, it becomes easier to control your flow of thoughts and emotions.

2: Separate your positive thoughts and feelings from the negative ones

Once you become mindful of your most dominant thoughts and feelings, you will be in a position to sieve your thoughts and separate the healthy from the unhealthy ones.

Imagine a deep hole beneath the surface of the earth where you can channel all thoughts that make building self-love challenging. Retain all positive thoughts and willingly replay them in your mind. You can make the positive thoughts into some kind of affirmations and repeat them as often as you can until they become a part of you.

3: Train yourself to become more mindful of what goes on around you

Making mindfulness a part of your daily life will increase self-love and the quality of life you live. Let us learn how you can make mindfulness a part of your daily life:

Practice Mindful Breathing

Mindful breathing is an aspect of mindfulness that helps you concentrate on how your breath cycles come and go. Mindful breathing begins with locating a suitable quiet spot free from any distractions. Anywhere around your home or office should be ideal provided the place is serene, secluded, and conducive to helping you easily master the art of concentration.

Once you find a location, settle into your most comfortable posture, and concentrate on your breathing taking in the whole whoosh sound as the air rushes in and out of your windpipe, the time it takes you to complete a cycle of breath, and how many breaths you can take in a minute. Do not think about anything else, only your breath matters at this point.

Develop a Mantra

A mantra is simply a word or sound you repeat severally to help you focus and concentrate during your mindful exercises. Your mantra can be a word, a phrase, sentence, or just a sound.

Developing and focusing on a mantra during your mindful exercises can help you become grounded/centered enough to notice the most lovable and amazing things about yourself and about life in general.

Your mantra can be one of the positive thoughts you created into an affirmation or any other thing you consider positive and motivating enough to make you love yourself more. It can be a thought centered on your major strengths and talents.

This mantra should form the basis of your focus as soon as you become accustomed to your breath and its pattern. Your mantra can be something like, "I'm the best singer, athlete, student, employee, best singer, actor, or investor."

Be mindful of everything else

The state of mindfulness should not stop at your breathing and mantra; you should be able to transfer it to every other activity you engage in during the day. These activities should include the ones you engage in at home and the ones you engage in when you are at the office or school.

When you take note of what goes on around you during the day, and how you handle issues that crop up in your line of work, the respect you have for yourself will grow, and naturally, your self-esteem will start on a bullish run.

Practice Self-Respect

Practicing self-respect is one of the most important aspects of practicing self-love. If you cannot respect yourself, it will be impossible to love yourself for who you are. You must find something to respect about yourself before you can find something to love about yourself. How can you practice self-respect? Here are some tips:

1: Carry yourself with dignity

The way you carry yourself tells a lot about how much you respect yourself and influences how people respect you.

Take queue from charismatic people and the way they carry themselves.

You can start by always walking briskly with your head held high and your shoulders squared. Even while seated, sit like someone who is sure of himself/herself by sitting straight with your legs stretched in front of you, hands clasped, and on your lap.

2: Present yourself in the most respectable way

There is a direct correlation between how you present yourself and how people address you. A great deal of how you present yourself has to do with what you wear and how you wear it. One school of thought says others address you depending on how you dress. This is something to maybe consider.

3: Have a high opinion of yourself

You do not need all the money, fame, or success in the world before you start seeing the royalty in you. Always treat yourself as if you have already attained the heights you are aiming for in life. Imagine the future you are working towards and see yourself there. This will increase your self-respect and self-love.

Chapter 4

KNOWING YOURSELF

Before you can practice self-love, you need to practice self-acceptance. To do so, you need to understand what self-acceptance is.

Self-acceptance involves accepting yourself for whom you truly are irrespective of your faults, weakness, and all. Self-acceptance means acknowledging your flaws and coming to terms with the fact that you have those flaws but understanding that these flaws do not have enough gravity to make you a failure in life. Self-acceptance is all about embracing your qualities and flaws and feeling satisfied and confident even when the odds are against you.

Self-acceptance precedes self-love. Practicing self-acceptance enables you to practice unreserved self-love. Once you accept yourself for whom you are, loving your flawed imperfect self becomes natural.

How can you practice self-acceptance to improve your self-love? Here are some steps you can take:

1: Weigh your strengths against your weaknesses

Get a piece of paper and a pen and use them to create something you can always refer to as a way to assess your progress. On one side of the paper, write everything you consider as your strengths, and on the other side of the paper, write everything you consider your strongest weaknesses.

2: Accept your weaknesses and commit to overcoming them

Once you make a list of your strengths and weaknesses, come to terms with the fact that you have some serious weaknesses to deal with and certain strengths you can leverage to make your life better.

It is not enough to accept you have certain weaknesses. You must also decide to work on them. If you do not try to get rid of your weaknesses, your many imperfections may make it hard for you to love yourself. For each weakness, set a goal to overcome it within a specified period, and never stop trying until you overcome that weakness.

3: Acknowledge your strengths and build upon them

It is easy to love yourself when you have several strong things going for you and life is good. Discovering your strengths and acknowledging them gives you several powerful reasons why self-love is something you have to pursue.

Your strengths are the things you discover you can do without waiting for anyone to teach or prompt you to do them. For instance, if you have the charisma to address large audiences and leave a lasting impression, then confidence is one of your greatest strengths.

4: Convince yourself you have all you need to live a great life

Philosophers have described the mind of man as a tabular slide. This means that your mind is an empty slate and whatever you write on it stays. If you start telling yourself you have all you need to be happy, fulfilled, and successful, your mind will easily believe that, and start working with that perspective as it seeks ways to make your dreams come true.

If you practice the above four steps, you should start wholly accepting the person you are, irrespective of your flaws and because you know your strengths, you will feel intricately motivated to pursue self-love, your goals, dreams, and aspirations.

Once this happens, you will be one-step closer to being a perennial self-lover.

Chapter 5

Developing Self-Compassion

The importance of self-compassion in our lives cannot be denied. Those who deny this reality and try to find effectiveness in excessive self-esteem and self-criticism or follow any other negative path in efforts of overcoming their problems, they are lead to the valley of desperation and anxiety by life. Nowadays due to extensive competition in every sphere of life, many people often get their focus diverted from their inner-self and their sole focus is on their worldly matters. As a result if they fail at any stage of their lives they are engulfed by epidemics of anxiety, loneliness, addiction and depression.

Social Anxiety Disorder:

It is usually observed that people who do not feel compassionate towards themselves are often involved in self-criticism. Many problems in social and personal life of a person can arise due to self-criticism and lack of self-compassion. The most common and alarming disorder that is caused due to these is known as Social Anxiety Disorder

(SAD) or Social Phobia. It falls in the category of mental disorders. In this type of disorder the subject unreasonably fears the social situations and their results. He is afraid of the criticism others might give him, in short he becomes negatively over-conscious about himself. All this anxiety can lead him to an attack of panic. He tends to run away from the realities of life and is in extreme distress. It is also suggested by studies that people who are suffering from SAD can't think clearly, have false beliefs and keeps negative opinion about others. Their public speaking skills are also rusted.

Academic Procrastination

It might be difficult to believe but people who are not self-compassionate are often procrastinators. A majority of such people are the students, who are at their crucial stages of life where self-compassion is needed the most. Procrastinators usually delay their important pieces of work and are indulged in pleasure seeking activities. Academic procrastination can lead to delay in home works, inability to complete important projects and assignments in time. It is not necessary for anyone to be in adversities to practice self-compassion. Self-compassion even in normal situations like daily academic routine is also useful; you can try to motivate your inner self to try to achieve the best possible outcome.

Increase in Depression

Depression is the most common type of disorder in the isolated and those that are affected and are living in adversities. Gender-wise depression is most common in women as compared to men. In depression a person thinks negatively about himself and the people around him; their perception about others is often negative and they tend to lose faith and trust in others. Many of these actions over a period of time can lead a person to depression; the most common of them is self-criticism. Beating ourselves up every time with self-criticism when we commit mistakes is a biggest mistake in itself. Instead of doing some good for you, it is likely to deteriorate motivation and the instinct of facing problems For those people who think that self-criticism is going to motivate you, to be honest self-criticism is quite painful and subconsciously, its outcome is the most dangerous. If you have seen someone who suffers from depression and examine their life style and their avour ur, you may get a clear picture of it.

Lack of Gratitude:

Lack of gratitude can be observed in people that are not compassionate towards themselves. In sufferings and adversities most part of our life is spent silently complaining to ourselves and others, this means that we are not grateful for what we have in hand. This leads us forget about the great thing that are currently present in our lives. Lack of gratitude in your personal life can increase your depression while in social life it can hurt your relationships with others.

Feeling Rushed

Lack of self-compassion can increase the feeling of urgency considerably. Throughout the day we experience a feeling of rushing on to the next task or thing. We want to move quickly, while working we tend to switch to next communication, next task, next tab etc. all of this is a constant source of stress and tension.

Distraction

Lack of self-compassion quite often results in distraction in everyday matters. Nowadays or live are super-distracted and we often waste our important time. This distraction obviously depicts the suffering in our lives, we do not want to complete our tasks because of the thoughts of failure. Distraction momentarily gives us comfort.

Rejection Sensitivity

Rejection sensitivity might be the most common problem in compassion-less people. We are actually afraid of the outcomes of the events and perceive different results and adapt ourselves to cope with the matters on the bases of our wrong expectations. Rejection sensitive people damage their interpersonal skills and are most likely to get involved in verbal hostility. Adolescent girls are most likely to have these problems as compared to the male gender.

Most of us here have done so many mistakes, some of it very dreadful, that we sometimes are unable to forgive even ourselves. A lot of times, it would come from other people, wherein they would be telling us that we've done something very wrong that they tell us we are unworthy of forgiveness. Us, lacking self-love, we choose to believe them. Doing so, we are basically giving ourselves permission to be miserable. We are giving the world an excuse that it is alright for us to suffer, more so, that it is natural for us to be experiencing negative things. A license to suffer so to speak.

But of course, before we can forgive ourselves, we must first have to admit that we have made a mistake, that we have done something wrong. Acceptance of our own imperfection. To tell ourselves it is okay that indeed we are capable of committing an error, just like everyone else.

Forgive ourselves for the fact that we are only human. We basically do not know everything at any given point in time. We are always open to making mistakes. People may condemn us or punish us for allowing ourselves to do so but that is very hypocritical of them. No one is perfect, that needs no reassurance. Every single person on Earth has made a mistake. Not even the greatest of personalities here on Earth are free of them, to which perhaps what have made them the greatest is the fact that they perhaps have made a million mistakes. Because the thing is, making a mistake shouldn't be a negative thing in the first place. It is good in the sense that it is through these mistakes that we are able to learn. These mistakes become the inspiration from where the next much better versions of ourselves will come from.

The most important thing is that we are humble enough to learn from these mistakes. This, in itself, is a form of self-love. It wouldn't matter if the whole world has already forgiven us for some mistake we have done, if we haven't forgiven ourselves yet for whatever it is that we have done wrong. To make it easier for us to imagine the benefits of forgiving ourselves, and simultaneously those around us, simply visualize that whenever we forgive, we also let go of an equivalent anchor that has been tied to our souls. Hence, the more that we do the act of forgiving, the more that our soul becomes lighter. Consider as well that forgiving is also the same as opening doors and windows that becomes pathways for blessings to come into our lives.

Forgiveness, as well, is the ultimate act of grace. Being able to pardon the mistakes of others and one's own mistakes, is something that is close to divinity. As the famous saying says that to err is human yet to forgive is divine. Only someone who has a truly generously loving heart and a mind full of understanding is capable of doing something close to a miracle. In contrast to when we choose to punish or condemn ourselves or those who have made mistakes. Just imagine, how someone would feel, if they were scheduled for death penalty on this very minute but then just seconds before execution, someone calls and announces that this person has been pardoned. By this analogy, forgiving yourself is like giving you a second chance at life. Whenever we are condemning ourselves it feels as if we aren't alive because our self-worth is so low.

Forgiveness then is most definitely an act of self-compassion. Being compassionate enough towards one's self that we choose to acknowledge the fact that we are simply humans capable of mistakes. Not only forgiveness for ourselves but for others, knowing especially that to forgive is not just an act we do for others but mostly for our own piece of mind. When we choose not to forgive, we choose instead to carry on hate, which then leads to anger. Such emotions that at this point we are already very aware is not really good for us mentally. Holding on to these things is like holding on to a bomb waiting to explode. So to be compassionate to ourselves.

Pride is something that doesn't let us forgive. Pride, which gives us this notion of having so much self-importance, allows us to think that we are incapable of making mistakes, hence making us incapable of seeing that we even need to forgive ourselves. More so, pride makes us feel that we are better than other people, it makes us arrogant to the point of thinking so highly of ourselves that we feel other people do not deserve our forgiveness. This completely goes against our self-compassion hence we must be thoroughly aware of our pride. Then of course make the conscious decision to rid ourselves of it. To forgive is to let go of pride, become more selfless, and put more emphasis and importance towards peace more than pride. Which is one of the things that we need most in the world right now. More and more people choosing to forgive instead of hate. More and more people choosing to hold flowers instead of bombs. Can you imagine a world that is more like this? There will be less hate, anger, and violence, and consequently means more peace, love, and unity. A more self-compassionate and self-loving world capable of making miracles, simply because we choose to forgive. Simply because we let go of what is unnecessary and focus instead on what we should truly value.

How many more relationships must fail because of our inability to forgive? Let us say no more. In the end, choosing not to forgive as we have mentioned only hurts us the most. So go on, let us do ourselves a avour and forgive. We most definitely deserve peace more than retribution.

Chapter 6

DEALING WITH EMOTIONS

Have you ever put anyone's needs before yours and found yourself resenting them for it after? This is a sign you were trying to be nice instead of truly kind. If you do not cover your own needs first, your resentment will inevitably grow towards the other person you helped out.. You may find you start passive-aggressive actions or snide remarks on your behalf. Resentment is what kills and often the other person can sense a type of aggressiveness from you towards them and are often oblivious to what they've done.

My friend John is a prestigious lawyer in America, he was talking to me about a pattern he found in a lot of domestic abuse cases. He said on his first case in this field how he walked in to talk to the suspect. Expecting to see an obviously violent man before him. He had seen the case reports and the horrific photographs of the woman who had been beaten. However when he walked in and started to interview the man in question he was shocked. The man was so friendly, nice and just seemed to be incapable of such a crime. So much so, John had to walk out and double-check if this was the right man he had seen sitting before him. John said over his long career, how he had seen a lot of cases exactly like this, and he couldn't understand the pattern. He then figured it out a theory for it one day. These men were so incapable of expressing their feelings or standing up for themselves that they suppressed it all. Them being nice caused them to receive years and years of abuse which they failed to deal with properly. The rage built up and built up until one day they snapped and all that rage, had to be released. This was not a healthy or kind way to deal with this problem and very badly affected the lives for all involved. When in a verbally abusive relationship like this man was, blame has to be put on both parties. If we don't speak up and stand up for ourselves, we encourage more of the same behavior from the abuser. In a lot of these cases, the men involved were victims who invited their abuse to a degree, when they didn't express how they felt. Which led from them being a victim, to becoming the abuser. It never would have happened if they had expressed how they really felt. If their wives continued this behavior, it was also their responsibility to leave. You see if we state we are not ok with something and the other person knows this and continues anyway, it is our responsibility to have the self-compassion to leave this person behind, as we don't need people like this in our lives. By doing this, showing yourself compassion, your self-esteem will be free to grow, if you don't, it will remain trapped amongst the thorns of your resentment.

Often being kind, is the hard thing to do but it is almost always the best thing to do.

Resentment Destroys Relationships and How To Deal With It

As we talked about before, resentment destroying relationships. If we fail to make clear boundaries how we expect other people to behave it is not their fault if they continue to act in a way you dislike. To help prevent resentment even being created in the first place, we must make sure our needs are covered before helping others. Once we do this, we help people from a place where we are centered and emotionally grounded.

The Contracts We Make In Our Heads

When putting others first we often unconsciously create a contract with that person in our heads. This contract should be disregarded however as only one party knows about it, that party is you. Nice people often have the tendency to do good things for others. However, this can often be followed by resentment for towards the person they helped. If you have ever felt this way, it was because you created a contract in your head. An example would be, say you have a friend who could do with losing weight. So you draw up a diet plan for them to follow and spend a good bit of time on it. A few weeks later, you find out they have not been following the diet plan, you feel a strong feeling of resentment towards them. If you feel this way, you were not coming from a truly kind place, as there is never resentment stemming from kindness. It is a lot more likely, coming from a place of being nice. A mindset of, "If I fix you, you have to like me." The contract in this situation was, "I'll draw up this diet plan, but you have to follow it." The only thing is the other person didn't know about this arrangement, it was never openly stated. This would have been different if before you had spent the time writing the plan out, you added conditions. If you were to say, "If I take the time to write this out for you, will you take it seriously and follow it?" This way the person will either agree or disagree. If they do agree and break the arrangement, at least they will have known they have, and you would simply not do something like this again for them. This way there are no hidden terms, and if the person doesn't follow the arrangement, it is openly known by both parties. The point here is not that you have to make everything into this deal format. It is that we should value our own time and if we are going to give it up for someone, it should be something that's important to them and they themselves take seriously. Otherwise, you are merely saying to yourself your time is less important than theirs. We also should allow people to help themselves or wait until they ask you for help. As this is coming from a much more emotionally centered place. Nice people often have a tendency to help someone who maybe hasn't asked for it or maybe doesn't even want it.

When we start to value our time, our self-esteem will consequently go up. When we recognize our own needs as important, it will raise our self-esteem. When we come from a place where we value our time, express what we would expect the other person to do as a result of our help, if there is anything, we can then help them out of a place of kindness and resentment-free.

Remember to monitor your feelings. If you feel resentment, ask yourself why and then take the appropriate action. It's often hard to look at our good deeds so critically, however, it is the best thing you can do for your relationships. If your friends or family care about you, they would rather you be honest with them than secretly going through periods of resenting them without their knowledge. Put yourself in their shoes, I don't know about you but I would rather my friends told me if they are not ok with doing something if it meant avoiding them resenting me. Then once we address the issue, our relationships get a lot stronger and more stable.

How We Talk To Ourselves

Words are powerful and can drastically change the way we perceive events. We are often our own harshest critics at a time where we need self-compassion. After our failures, we often go through long periods of reliving the events in our head unable to let go of them. What makes this worse is what we chose to focus on and the words we use when we speak to ourselves. There is a place for the use of this pain to motivate us to do better. However, there are times when we need to show compassion to ourselves and sometimes do what is hardest of all and forgive ourselves.

Often we speak to ourselves worse than we would speak to our worst enemy. However nothing beneficial comes of this, instead we need to take responsibility for what we say to ourselves. When we take control of this, talk to yourself as you would to a close friend going through the same ordeal. Often people will say they need this abuse as motivation, however it had exactly the opposite than the desired effect. When we are too harsh of critics, it leads to depression mind states which make it difficult to do or achieve anything difficult. Whereas if we are encouraging to ourselves we can use this as fuel for motivation and for change in our life, if we see fit.

When an event we did not desire has happened, it can be hard to let go of. Even years down the line, we still carry this pain with us, unable to let it go and forget it. We can only ever learn from our mistakes, however it makes no sense to carry the pain on with us as we move forward with our lives. To do this, first we need to acknowledge and accept these events happened. One of the easiest ways to do this is to write it down on a piece of paper. Then once you have accepted, they have happened and have written it down, tear up the piece of paper. This sounds stupid and illogical, however, the thing with our emotions and dealing with them is that they are often illogical. It's amazing how effective this little trick is and I urge you to try it.

We also have a tendency to feel isolated when we're not feeling too good. We feel as if we are the only one that feels this way, however that is never the case. There is a famous saying, "The more personal a problem, the more universal it is." When we're feeling low, we can force ourselves to remember other people feel like this as well and if others can get through it, so can we. It's ok to feel this way, it's just a sign we may need to change something in our lives. It is important to know we are never alone.

Self-Acceptance Exercise

In this exercise, we will work with accepting ourselves in this present moment for who we are, faults and all. It should be practiced over the course of a couple of weeks. There is a kind of paradox in this area of self-help, as in one aspect you are accepting yourself for who you are and in the other, you are trying to improve yourself. However the way I deal with this is, as long as I am working on being my best self, then I can accept myself as I am. This way you grow and learn to accept yourself for the way you are.

It's remarkable how much a small change on your inside can have such a profound influence on your life and external reality as a whole. Our mind influences our outside world, and this is where we need to change to get long lasting significant results. The external is often a superficial side, a bi-product of what is going on inside.

Ok to start off, put your attention in this present moment. Pay attention to the sensations in your body and notice how they feel. Pay attention to your breathing. Feel the air going past your lips, notice if the air is warmer or colder as it comes out from your lungs past your lips. Now I want you to bring up a time where you felt love for a person or an event. Feel that sensation throughout your body. Extend it throughout your body. Now take this love and apply it to the other parts of your personality. Think of the part of you that's funny, apply it to that side, don't logically think of what you are doing, just doing it. Give this part of your personality your complete undivided unconditional love. Now take the part of your personality that feels shame, conjure up that feeling and then give your undivided unconditional love towards this part of your personality. Now bring up the part of your personality that has overreacted with anger towards something, and give your unconditional love to this part of your personality.

Now continue to do this for all the different parts of your psychology. I'll list some here:

- ❖ The part of you that has felt embarrassed.
- ❖ The part of you that has a high work ethic.
- ❖ The lazy part of you.
- ❖ The sad part of your psychology.
- ❖ The happy part of your psychology.
- ❖ The part of you that has felt rejected.
- ❖ The part of you that is sexually frustrated.
- ❖ The part of you that is confident.
- ❖ The part of you that has felt guilty.

And any others you can think of.

Continue to regularly do this whenever you have any free time, and you'll be amazed how your psychology will change in a few weeks. You are wholeheartedly accepting yourself, flaws and all.

Self-Forgiveness

More often than not the hardest person for us to forgive is often ourselves. We can have so much trouble letting go sometimes even when it's of no help to anyone. All we can do is learn from our mistakes. Here I will show you how to learn to forgive yourself.

So to deal with guilt we must understand why we feel it. We feel guilt due to two reasons: We believe that our actions have caused a bad result and that we were responsible for that result. So in order to deal with guilt, we need to change at least one of these.

Us as humans haven't developed the Godlike ability to predict exactly what will happen due to our actions. We are limited in that way. So thus we cannot be held responsible for that result as it is out of our control. This is especially true if you set out with good intentions.

We also don't know the ramifications of our actions further down the line. By us causing a bad event to happen in someone's life, we could be leading them onto a path of something better down the road. Your actions could lead them to find the love of their life or be happier than ever.

We never really know the full scale of events that happen to us in our lives. So thus we can't competently claim that our actions have led to a bad result.

I am not saying to never take responsibility, what I am saying is guilt often serves no purpose after an initial phase. We must merely, set out with good intentions, learn from our actions and try to implement our new found knowledge in future decisions.

Building Unshakable Self-Esteem

Many of us derive our self-esteem from achieving certain results or feeling better than someone. It is the norm in our society that being average is actually bad. If you called someone average, they would be more than likely offended. So for a lot of us, we derive our self-esteem from us being better than other people. However this is a foolish way to view life. We were born with self-esteem, it is our natural state, however, more often or not, certain influences on our life have drilled it out of us.

So how do we start to regain our self-esteem? I've talked about in the previous chapters, however here I want to add something which I believe to be absolutely crucial to not only self-esteem but long term sustainable self-esteem. It is living a life of principles, rather than a life of results. Having a high work ethic for your job is a principle. Getting promotions is a result. Having good intentions is a principle, people liking you due to something you did for them is a result. More often than not, living by principles will gear you towards your result. However we must remember a lot of life is out of our control, the only thing we can control is our actions.

An example of a person, living a life by results would be: Say you set out to help someone, however, something out of your control went wrong, and it ended up causing them more hassle instead of helping them. Often people would take this very badly, and it would negatively affect their self-esteem. However, someone with a principle-based self-esteem wouldn't take this badly. As you had good intentions, you were not knowledgeable or in control of what happened so don't feel bad about it. If it is necessary, surely apologize to the person. However don't view yourself as a bad person because something bad has happened. After it has happened, definitely learn from your mistakes and use that knowledge to decide how you would do it differently the next time but don't get hung up on it. This would be entirely different if you set out with bad intentions, however. This is where integrity comes into play. We always know what the right thing to do is. We should always follow this feeling no matter what, as otherwise, we compromise our integrity and thus our self-esteem. It can be easy standing up for what you believe to be right a lot of the time but sometimes it is extremely difficult, and so these are the times that matter the most.

To live a life of principles, we must first know what are principles are. It is worth spending time writing these down and writing down what we believe in. Even knowing these principles will make a massive difference to our lives. So often we can be put in a situation where we have to think so fast that we make a decision we later regret. It is a lot easier when you know who you are and what you stand for, however. Once you know the principles in your life that you follow, then follow them no matter what. Integrity is a vital part of how we view ourselves. So start taking the importance of the results you get and focus on living a life of integrity by following your own core principles.

Chapter 7

THE POWER OF SELF-COMPASSION

Nowadays we might not have enough time to sit down and talk to ourselves. Our lives have become so complicated that we do not know what we are chasing, why are we wasting our time and what do we want. All we are taught is to be successful and lead a content life but we are never told what successful life means and what sort of life is the best. We work day and night in order to find that success and eventually we start to realize that we have been on the wrong path and we have been after the mistaken ambitions of life. The result is that we end up in adversities and it's too late to go back and change the past. We are beaten by ourselves to our knees and getting up seems to be impossible in such adversities.

At such adverse stages of life it is quite natural that we think of ourselves to be failures and we are often jealous of other people out there that are having a good time while you suffer. So at this stage thinking that we are the ones n problem and showing self-pity towards oneself is a foolish thing. This leads to many misleading thoughts, self-criticism and sometime people give up their efforts. They are indulged in self-sabotage and distress. The anxieties are ever increasing and the amount of stress on us is quite alarming. We think that this is the end of life, but wait this is not.

In Asian cultures, man is considered to be a sculpture made out of mistakes. Everyone makes mistakes and somehow it is our nature to feel regret over them. The point here to ponder is that no one knows what the future holds for them and no sensible person would commit mistakes willingly. Everything that happens is our fate. If we had the ability to know about the future, no one would commit mistakes. Everyone would have been perfect and flawless.

Actually this is not the case and mistakes and the subsequent sufferings are a part of everyone's life. Our imperfections lead us to the adversities and sufferings. But our imperfection is not to be blamed because we have to live with the notion that everyone can commit mistakes and no one can lead a happy life forever. Our main focus after admitting these facts should be not to give up and keep on doing our efforts to fend off the problems and sufferings and try to achieve some harmony in our lives. To deal with your negative problems in some positive way is the beauty of self-compassion.

At these stages of life the most suitable companion that can help you regaining confidence, willpower and a regain a sense of purpose in life, is self-compassion. Admitting our shortcomings and still trying to keep ourselves on the move are nothing less than valor and bravery. Moreover the sufferings and challenges give a meaning to life.

The human progress towards stability is not something that happens overnight, rather it is a progressive, stable and genuine advance towards the peaks of life. We cannot expect to get out of the downs of life overnight, instead it takes will power, vision, endurance, patience and last but not the least self-compassion. The main conclusion is that admitting ones mistakes, considering sufferings to be a part of life and doing the utmost efforts to get up on your feet and face the adversities is quite a difficult task in itself, but those who are upto this task are the ones who emerge out successful.

How many times have we concerned ourselves with the past or the future? Lost sleep over these things that really do not exist in the first place? It may be hard to believe for some, but think about it, the past and the future are merely figments of our imagination. Many of us having experienced anxiety over the thought of something horrible that happened in the past, or something equally as terrible in the future, can relate very well to what I'm saying. Sometimes, we think these two things are so real we let it affect us to a certain degree. The most common perhaps is not being able to sleep thinking about a past scenario wherein something unpleasant happened to us, or imagining a future event wherein we think about something truly disastrous that would happen. Since usually this happens when we are about to sleep and relax, but our mind says something else, and keeps playing these scenes in our head, as if it were happening right that moment. Right now, if we were to think about a past or future event, notice very well that it is only happening inside of our minds. The past and future in essence are merely illusions, projections of the mind.

Whenever we think about a past or a future situation, we have to deeply realize within ourselves that it is but an illusion. It's just that sometimes whenever we are thinking about a past or a future situation, depending on what we are imagining, it can be quite overwhelming for us hence we are pulled into that chain of thought. But if we try to relax ourselves and see these situations as they are, illusions, it loses its power over us and we become capable of taking a step back and stop ourselves from imagining these situations. Thinking about the past and the future is simply a program we have embedded within our minds as a means to warn of us negative things that have happened in the past and may happen in the future for us to be able to prevent them in the present. In other words, they are simply warning signs, no more no less. Except, what happens to us is that we accept these supposed to be warning signs more than they should be, we believe them to be real right that exact moment we are thinking about them hence they affect us when really they should not.

Our projections of the future themselves are a form of memory, for most of the time we simply base them on past events. For example, we think that we are going to fail in the future basing it on a past event wherein we have also failed. We must be vigilant that what happens in the present depends mostly on what we do in the present, not memories of the past and the future. We have to be aware that everything is simply an outcome of how we deal with the present moment.

Our main focus for this chapter, is for us to become grounded in the present moment, that which we also call "now". Consider, that if we are unperturbed by thoughts of the past and the future, what is always left is this present moment. And within this present moment, coupled with awareness, we find we aren't as miserable as our thoughts of past and future lead us to be. Relating it to the idea of suffering, we suffer because focusing on the past and future is to focus on the things we do not already have, considering these things are just basically figments of our imagination. In contrast to focusing on the present moment, wherein we are able to focus on the things we already have. More specifically, the power that we have within us to direct what we can and not do during this specific moment. Isn't it so? Right now, we can most definitely choose what we wish to do. Although perhaps there can be limitations depending on each of our situations and status in life, but the most important thing is the fact that we are able to choose. That choice in itself is the ultimate power that the present moment gives us. And the more that we exercise that power to choose, the more that we are able to practice it. That being said, within this moment, choose to simply become aware and you become more and more aware. Consequently, the more that we become alive.

Now, if we think about it, we will finally realize that the only time we every really have is always this "now" moment. There was never really a time that we have lived anywhere else in time but now. And from this point on we should be completely aware of the fact that the past and future are merely concepts that we have of time. Forms of memories that we only think up in our minds that distracts us from the present moment, and the more that we separate ourselves from the present moment, the more that we open ourselves into suffering, into states of being away from self-love and self-compassion. Perhaps, you might ask, what if you are thinking about a past or a future memory in which there is the presence of self-love or self-compassion. What of it? Both still focuses on the idea that during the current moment there is no self-love or self-compassion and instead we look for them within these memories.

Hence, instead of fantasizing over illusory moments of past and future, we must be constantly aware of the present moment. For us to be able to consistently create and open ourselves to the infinite possibilities and opportunities that is available to us always within the present moment. The only time we can ever create and manifest real and concrete actions that enables or moves us towards the things that we want. We cannot have true peace and concrete moments of self-compassion or self-love just imagining it in our minds, we have to create it constructively within the reality of the present moment, and there is no other way around it. It will not go away, in fact we are only running away from these problems if we are only going to live in thoughts of past and future. So, I deeply urge you, be here, now. Claim the power that is within the present moment and from this create for yourself the reality that you truly want. The such displeasing thoughts of scenarios of past and future are simply guides that point us towards the present moment that we truly want. They are far from real, only if we act upon them can they become real.

So far, a lot of what we discussed, all boils down to these two motivating forces, which is fear and love. Every time we listen to a negative thought, and let it consume us, fear is what we are listening to. Every time we worry over something, isn't it fear written all over it? Fear that something bad is going to happen. Fear that we are going to lose something. Fear that we are underserving of something. Fear that we are not going to make it, that we are going to fail. Fear that we are not going to be accepted and Fear of what other people think.

Every negative thing in this world stems down to fear. While every positive thing branches out from love. Realize, that if we are being directed by fear more than love, we also direct ourselves to live miserable and pathetic lives. Instead of us going after the things we want in life, we go ahead and become the number one antagonist in our lives by believing that we can't make it ourselves. We feel fear that we do not have the necessary gifts to do what we want. We fear that we are going to fail. We fear that the things that we want are impossible to achieve and cannot be done. So, if we let go of these fears, and have the courage to choose love instead, love in the sense that we believe in ourselves enough to have faith that we are capable of achieving the things that we want, we become our greatest ally. More so, being capable of believing in ourselves is a most wonderful act of love and compassion towards one's self. This way, in contrast to listening to our fears where we already give up on ourselves even though we haven't even tried yet, being able to give ourselves a chance at succeeding simply because we take the courage to at least try is already worth so much. Yes, indeed it is a possibility that we may fail, there are a lot of reasons why it's going to be really hard, but we are simply going to ignore these things more so because failure is not the end of the world but just a speed bump in life.

Our relationship with other people are also greatly affected by the play between fear and love. If we are being led by fear, our trust and affection towards other people also significantly decreases. We are afraid to trust or love other people because we fear that they are going to disappoint us. We fear that they are not going to love us back or return our trust. Whether it is a personal or a business relationship, we are not given room to thrive because we let fear command us and our actions. Hence, for us to have a beautiful thriving relationship not just with ourselves but the people around us, we must learn to let go of fear. Or more appropriately, we must learn to have the proper courage to face these fears. To have so much courage that we are capable of saying, so what if I fail? So what if they disappoint me? So what if things may go wrong? So are all the things im striving for worth it anyway? That's right, loving ourselves enough is also synonymous to tough love, we must be willing to go through hardships and failures just so we can give ourselves the things that we love, things that we very much deserve. Realize that love is truly at the other side of fear. If we cross that beyond our fears, we find love and every beautiful thing that also comes with it, peace, happiness, abundance, and much more.

Furthermore, connecting it with everything that we have conferred up to now, fear and love is a present factor in all of them. First and foremost, with regards to suffering, we have discussed that what makes us suffer is the idea of losing something, hence that is basically the fear that we feel whenever we are threatened to lose something. It may not be the direct solution to the upcoming threat that we are about to lose something, but it is the most effective way we are going to be able to push through and more efficiently successfully acquire more of whatever that is that we are losing at the current moment. Better that we are working on what we want calm and composed than to go about panicking and worrying which considerably lessens our chances at being successful.

Next, one of the main reasons or perhaps the only reason we choose not to forgive, as we have previously discussed, is pride. Now, pride as a reason why we choose not to forgive is practically also an offspring of fear.

Whenever we choose not to bestow forgiveness upon ourselves or another that is because we fear that we are not getting the respect and love that we deserve, hence we respond with such displeasure and so we say, "No, I cannot forgive you". But we if already give to ourselves the love and respect that we do deserve, we do not need to deprive anyone of forgiveness anymore for we are already fulfilled from within. It is also pretty much the same situation whenever we choose not to give ourselves self-love.

Lastly, when it comes to choosing our self-identity, what stops us from adapting the highest form of self-reflection, the idea of "I am", is of course, fear. As well as the idea of transcending from the body and towards the soul. We cannot adapt these ideas because we fear it is not possible. We think "I am only this body, it is impossible for me to become the soul" and so we choose to stay as the body. But if we truly want to we can rid ourselves of that certain fear and choose instead these more advanced forms of being simply because it is what gives us a deeper sense of meaning and peace.

So, no matter how crippling and influential our fears may be, always have the courage to choose love. Do not listen to these haunting screams of fear and instead open your ears to the beautiful melody that love plays for us. To listen to fear is to give up on the possibility of the good things in life, doing so we automatically revoke our right towards achieving, but if we listen to love and at least try, we increase our chances at a very large percent. Even if at the times that we fail, the fact that at least we have tried, gives us a sense of fulfillment no amount of fear can ever give us. Love yourself enough to decide that we are worthy and deserving of the life that we want regardless of the fear that we may not achieve it

Here in this chapter we are going to magnify on the interdependence of our thoughts, emotions, and actions. To accentuate on just how powerful these things are as influences in our lives. This idea has already been presented in our other chapters but here we are going to expand on it much more comprehensively. Let us start with our thoughts, which are basically the starting point of everything that happens into our lives. For all of us who are believers of God, we can actually say that the creation of the world in itself was actually ignited because God thought of creating us. In essence then, the world, the universe, is basically God's idea manifested into reality. Now, if that is not enough evidence especially if you're not a believer of God, let us instead consider everything else in the world which is made by man. A radio, a television, your high-end laptop, the vehicle that you drive, up to the simple handkerchief that we use to wipe our faces with, these things are all basically inventions of man that actually started as an idea. Someone thought about them and decided to follow that thought and try to create an exact copy of that idea into reality. Many of course have somehow failed getting their ideas to manifest, but look at the world now filled with so many successful ideas that have turned into real concrete things that we can actually see, hold, and experience. This is exactly why in the starting chapters we have so vigorously highlighted on being able to control our thoughts. Starting with self-awareness which allows us to become conscious of our thoughts. Talking about the idea of suffering and of past and future as ideas that creates illusions in our minds and hinders us from being able to take control of our own thoughts. Up to the concept of meditation which basically completes the process, allowing us the opportunity of fully regaining control over our minds and consequently our thoughts.

To which now, having controlled our thoughts, or at least having been enlightened on just how important it is for us to have control over our thoughts, let us start to discuss more extensively about our emotions. For in a way we actually have already discussed about this in our earlier chapters and to be more specific, the effects of our thoughts towards our emotions. If you have not realized by now, self-compassion, self-love, forgiveness, and most especially, suffering, are actually forms of emotions. These things are basically emotions that we feel that stems or originates from our thoughts. Self-compassion, to start with, is basically an emotion that we feel whenever we think about having sympathy and concern for ourselves. It is what we feel whenever we are moved by the idea of ourselves experience some sort of suffering or misfortune. If in the first place, we did not have any idea of what suffering or misfortune is, we wouldn't feel self-compassion towards ourselves in the first place, nor compassion for other people. If we did not have an idea of what it is like to feel pain, isn't it that we would actually feel indifferent towards it? If we did not have the idea or the knowledge that people who have not eaten for days would feel extremely hungry, we would not feel one single bit of empathy towards them at all. Let alone if we did not know what being hungry is about in the first place. To give another example, let us also talk about forgiveness. The idea of forgiveness, to begin with, is very much connected to the idea or thought that someone has wronged or harmed us. If, in actuality, we did not have the concept that we are actually capable of being wronged or harmed by others, then we are not going to feel hate towards anyone in the first place. There is no one to forgive right from the start, yet, since we have such an idea, we then are capable of feeling hate or displeasure towards others hence we are also capable of feeling or it is necessary for us to also feel forgiveness towards others. To make things even clearer, let us now also mention suffering. Isn't it, as we have discussed, that suffering is basically something that we feel whenever we think that we are losing something or in a way when we think that harm is being done to us? If, in the beginning, we did not have the idea of what suffering is like in the first place, then do you think we are still going to feel such suffering? Now, for us to have a clearer understanding of the connection between our thoughts and emotions, let us now also discuss the feeling of happiness. Isn't it so that we become happy whenever we think of the things that we think are beneficial for us? Like for example having delicious food to eat, a nice warm home to stay in, or simply having enough air to breathe. Thoughts of having these things can't help but put a smile on our faces. Being in complete contrast to when we complain, despite already having these blessings in our lives, complaining that somehow they are still not enough, we then consequently suffer. Which of course, as we are more aware of now, is basically stems from thinking that the things we have are not enough for us. Being more acquainted now of the power of our thoughts towards our emotions, isn't it that we now feel more conscious and are now more inclined towards being more responsible when it comes to our thoughts? That thoughts do not only cause physical manifestations to come about in our lives but as well as emotional manifestations. Knowing about this now, we are given the opportunity to be able to experiment and explore the vast plethora of emotions that we are capable of feeling as humans or simply as sentient beings. We can now mix and match certain emotions with specific thoughts basically allowing us the power to choose which emotions we would like to feel during a certain moment. This skill, at first, is going to be really hard to master let alone control, especially if we only just have started realizing that we actually do have such power or skill, but overtime, like with everything else, constant practice allows us to become more proficient at it.

Lastly, let us now discuss the effects of our thoughts and emotions towards our actions. Actions like our emotions, also originates from our thoughts, moreover, at the same time, is also influenced by our emotions. As a simple example, whatever it is that we are doing now, is basically motivated by some specific idea that allows us to think that we should be doing it right now. As a concrete example, as I am writing this book, I am practically intoxicated by the idea that by all means, I should be writing this book right now, as of this very moment. I could be doing something else, but no, the main idea that is stuck in my mind right now is the idea of finishing this book, and so I write. You, who is currently reading this book right now, is most likely compelled by some idea that reading this book as of this moment is the best thing that you can do as of this moment. Perhaps supported by some idea that within this book you will find something very important, hence why you are reading it. With regards to emotions, which a lot of times have been a very powerful motivation towards our actions, you are reading right now because most possibly you feel good about reading something right now, or perhaps looking at it from another perspective, you actually feel sad and so you read this book because somehow it makes you feel good. On that context, most of the time, we actually do the things that we do because they are the things that make us feel good or positive. Someone intentionally working towards feeling negative may be a very unlikely phenomenon, but if in such case, the point is, whatever negative emotion that is that he or she wants to move forward to, the fact remains that he or she has willed to achieve such emotion. If, in the case where one is unconsciously moving towards a certain negative emotion, then that is one of the main purposes of this book, for one to be made aware of such things – that indeed there will be times that we become unaware that we ourselves are causing ourselves to feel negative emotions, which has been mentioned and inevitably will be mentioned many more times in this book in many ways. Anyway, back to our actions basically being the results of our thoughts or emotions, one of our goals is to consequently become highly aware of such fact. At certain point in our lives, such unawareness in this area may prove to be very unpleasant for us. The best example for this may come from actions that we do that originates from incessant thoughts and emotions of anger. How many times have we done something very destructive towards others and most especially towards ourselves just because we have acted out of fury? I know a lot of us here have done something very terrible just because we have let our anger take control of us and our actions. This perhaps is what we should be most wary of. As such, it is very important that we may be able to discern with pinpoint accuracy which thoughts and emotions are most beneficial for us. In little doses, it may prove to be unimportant, but overall, what becomes of our lives is ultimately the summation of all the thoughts that we have thought, emotions that we have felt, and actions that we have done.

That being said, as of this moment, whether you like or do not like wherever you are now, then it is most likely because of a certain thought, emotion, or action. Moreover, as we have been graciously pointing out, these things are within our control. If in the case that you do not like where you are now, then perhaps now is the time to take the time to be aware of whatever thought, emotion, or action, is driving you to be where you are now, for you to finally redirect yourself towards where you want to be, or more importantly who you want to be, and ultimately, how you want to be. At this point of the book, we have already discussed much of what we need to know to be able to do just that, much more so now that we are even more aware of the power of our own actions, in relation to our emotions and our thoughts – specifically, following the positive thoughts and emotions that bring about highly satisfactory and fulfilling results. With that, let us now, with steadfast and unwavering awareness, move on to the next chapter.

Chapter 8

OVERCOME YOUR PAST

Turning weaknesses into strengths

Society always hammers in our head from childhood to focus on our weaknesses (not that it's wrong) but it should also go along with focusing on your strengths as well. We spend our whole lives just dwelling on what we are not good at or lack that we forget to focus on what we excel at.

E.g. Zack is weak at math but he writes excellent poetry and short stories. But his parents and teachers always tell him how bad he is at math and that he can't progress in life if he doesn't score well in math. He then gets disheartened thinking he can't do anything or that he's not smart enough and even stops writing poetry.

Accept your weaknesses

A lot of people in the pursuit of success are in this state of denial when it comes to their weaknesses and in doing so they end up failing more. There is no harm in accepting your weaknesses. It is not going to make you any lesser of a person in doing so.

Once you acknowledge your weakness it will be easier for you to improve it or move past it. Accepting your weaknesses helps you to make more room for improvement and gives you a reason to grow more and expand your consciousness.

Get good enough at them

So let's go back to Zack's example, he was weak at math but that does not mean he should also give up math completely and just pursue his writing. He should take extra lessons and practice hard in math just enough to get a decent grade in it. Just because you have a weakness does not mean you let it stay a weakness for ever. Conquer them if they are important for you. Just like in Zack's case because he had to pass the SATs.

Hire your weaknesses

Sometimes you got to hire people who are skilled in things you are not good at. It saves you time, effort and the frustration. Nobody in this world is perfect in everything and sometimes the best thing for you to do is to partner up with someone who is better at it. Synergizing to create a better result is the way to go!

Nobody is free from failure in this life. Your failures make your or break depending on what your perception is. You might have often seen successful people but never would have imagined what hardships or failures they had to go through to achieve that level of success. This is because it is impossible to have accomplished so much without ever experiencing failure.

If you ever want to know about some of these successful people then read about Walt Disney, Jack Ma, Winston Churchill, Steve Jobs etc and you will realize that failure is nothing but a phase of life that everyone goes through.

J.K Rowling was giving a commencement speech to Harvard students and guess what did she talk about? Not success but failure. Imagine giving a speech to a crowd of students who have known nothing but success in life and studying in one of the best institutions of the world being given an important life lesson: Failure. One of her most well-remembered quotes from that speech was:

Accept your failures

If you have failed in life no matter how big or small, just accept them. There is no point staying in a state of denial or in a sinking feeling of guilt and blame.

Failing is not being able to succeed in life. Failing is not being able to succeed and not trying again or do anything about it. It is simply planting the seeds of success.

Intrinsically, if we are going to decipher that emotion that we call "happiness", it is simply an emotion that correlates deeply with how we view our lives, and that is whether we do not have enough of the things that we need and want in life, or if we have more than enough. Of course, if we think that we have many of the things that we need and desire, then we become happy.

Being able to live in the moment, without fear, we find this amazing clarity that allows us to become impressively grateful within our lives. For having this clarity, unperturbed by fearful thoughts of the past and future, we can see that within the moment there is already so much to be thankful for. The air that we breathe in itself is something that we have to be highly grateful for. Something that perhaps we take so much for granted thinking it's only natural for us being able to breathe air. But think about it, there are so many planets present in our universe, or within our galaxy alone, but it is only Earth that has enough oxygen in the air for it to be capable of supporting life. The planet, moreover, is also something we can be thankful for. Think about it, releasing ourselves from thoughts of fear, and grounding ourselves to the present moment, everything as in everything we can find becomes something to be thankful for. Crazy as it may seem, but even our problems are worth being grateful for. Think about how without these problems, we wouldn't be able to grow and become better versions of ourselves. Realize that it is mainly because of these problems that have we learned to give ourselves more love and compassion.

Now, as we have discussed, suffering is simply the state of being in which we are directing our focus towards the things that we are losing during a certain a moment. Gratitude is basically the exact opposite of that. Whenever we are being thankful, isn't it that during that time we are thinking of something that we already have in our life and feeling appreciative of it? Now, if we are going to analyze, during any moment, as long as we are alive, there is always, and I mean always, something to be thankful for. Considering now that we have exercised meditation and have achieved self-control especially over our thoughts, we are now highly capable of choosing any specific thought within any moment. Which also means we are now also less bothered by unwanted thoughts that bring about negative responses from within us as the techniques we have learned allows us to skillfully just redirect such negative thoughts into positive ones. That being so, we are then capable of directing our focus towards things that we can be thankful for. With this, we acquire the ability to always be thankful no matter what situation we are in.

Now, the most beautiful thing about gratitude is that it is basically a magnet for more things to be thankful for. The idea is that when we train our minds to always look for things to be thankful for, no matter what the situation is, then we'll always be able to find something to be thankful for. As we practice it more and more, it is like a muscle that also becomes more and more powerful. Unlike when we use our minds to always look for the negative in any situation, isn't it that we also always find something to be negative about? Thereby making us suffer. So which would we rather choose? Of course, we should rather be thankful. A lot of the time whenever we complain about a situation it's because we do it unconsciously. In addition, we are not aware of the effects of complaining hence we go on complaining about things that do not go in our favor. Which ironically makes things a lot worse than it actually is. Now, that we are aware of it, it would be much easier to get a hold of ourselves and stop this habit of complaining and redirect ourselves towards the right path of gratitude.

Gratitude is also the most effective way of making the things we value stay in our lives for the longest time possible. When we feel gratitude towards the things that we love, it is like we are creating an imaginary glue that binds us to them.

The more that we feel gratitude and appreciation, the more that the things that we already have stick to us. To make this idea easier to visualize, let us again discuss the opposite of it. Whenever we complain about the things that we already have, isn't it that after some time these things somehow find a way to leave us? Especially with people, whenever we keep complaining about their presence in our life, isn't it that after some time they would eventually leave? Simply because we did not appreciate them. Of course, anything or anyone that is not appreciated, would not want to stay around us. For whenever we complain to people, it is very much like we are telling them that we do not want them in our life. As humans, one of our most basic needs is the need to be appreciated. Hence, whenever someone in our life does not feel appreciated, they would eventually leave so they could find someone else who would generously appreciate them. Which of course also works with material things. I've experienced many times having lost a material possession just because I did not appreciate it. The most concrete example is when we fail to take care of our material possessions, which is basically a way of saying that we do not value them, and so overtime, not being well taken care of they eventually get broken. How many times have we regretted not being able to appreciate something that we had in our life only after when it's gone?

So we come back to appreciation or gratitude. In the most basic sense, feeling grateful towards the things that we value is our way of taking care of them, most especially our relationship with them. Going out of our way to let them know we appreciate them every day, our relationship with them strengthens and so, like we mentioned, they become attached to us as if they were glued to us. Consequently, we become more at peace and happy not just within ourselves but outside ourselves. Speaking of which, in the first few chapters, we have been basically learning how to become appreciative of ourselves. Which again involves self-awareness, self-empathy and self-love. When we are constantly self-aware we are basically giving ourselves consistent attention, which much like appreciation is also a basic need. Doing these things we are able to create a very healthy relationship within ourselves consequently becoming our greatest source of peace and happiness. Our relationship with others are simply secondary. No matter how good our relationship are with those that are around us, in the end, as we have already been made aware of, our constant companion would be ourselves.

For us to be always appreciative towards ourselves is like always having a friend we can turn to for love and affection. Hence, being able to do so, we become the number one thing that we can always be thankful for no matter the situation. This way, being thankful all the time has become a constant possibility, for now you can always say within yourself, "I am thankful I have me." With such perspective, again, it doesn't matter if the world may crumble nor if the people you trust the most are not around. You are constantly able to rely on yourself even to your most basic of needs. Consequently, being able to do so, we are capable of appreciating even more then what we receive from another. Making us significantly more grateful, and such it also can't be helped that we also become much happier.

Let failure free you

People are afraid of failing so much that they live all their lives worrying not to fail instead of focusing on the actual possibility of success. Allow yourself the margin to fail because if you go through it, it will set you free from all the fears and worries. It will make you stronger and move ahead on life easily.

Learn from them

Your failures and mistakes in life are not there to break you or to depress you. In fact, they are there to make you come out much stronger and help you to realize where all your strengths lie.

Make Plan B's and C's

Just because one way of reaching your goal didn't pan out the way you wanted it to be does not mean you give up and not try it any other way. Make another plan or different strategy to achieve those goals. E.g. if you can't afford to go to the college of your choice or didn't get hired from the company of your choice then know that it is nothing personal against you and that you can find a better opportunity elsewhere.

Accept that certain things are not good for you

Sometimes life throws you a curveball and makes you realize things that didn't work out for you or you failed at were actually blessings in disguise. You then understand that you were meant to pursue other things that were better for you. Trust the universe and know that everything is always working in your favor.

Take responsibility for your life

Once you grow up and become an adult, you can no longer blame anyone for the problems in your life. Even if they were caused by other people, you can't give them the power to ruin your happiness. You should find ways to fix the problems in your life calmly and maturely instead of playing the blame game. Successful people always take 100% responsibility for their lives and so should you.

Embrace the pain

Don't run from failures or pains in life because you are only setting yourself up for huge disappointments. Look them all in the eye and face them with courage because only then will the pain become lesser and be reduced down to nothing.

I hope now you can finally understand that failure is a part of life that should not only be accepted but to be openly talked about. Failure shouldn't be people don't think of it as something shameful to discuss. Who knows you could be an inspiration to someone later on?

Chapter 9

Physiology of Self-Compassion

As we see now, much of the things that affects us can be found internally, not externally. Specifically, our thoughts. Hence, now, the importance of being able to classify the role of our minds in our lives. If we would analyze, as we have been discussing in the past chapters, our thoughts are basically what influences us most during any kind of situation. Which leads us to the conclusion that if we are able to take control of our thoughts, then we are also able to take control over our composure or our emotions. If we observe further, it is primarily because of our lack of control over our minds that we are able to experience a lot of negative emotions. Whenever we let our minds take control and bombard us with negative thoughts we become crippled. Every time we allow it to do so means we are consciously forgetting that we are the ones that should be in control. We are surrendering ourselves to our own weaknesses. The mind is practically the filter we use as to what we're going to choose to allow what comes into our lives. Whether we're going to subscribe to thoughts infested with fear or thoughts charged with love. So, much of what we need to do, is being able to have self-control enough to be able to direct the thoughts that we wish to have. To remember that the mind is our servant and we are the master not the other way around. To be able to realize that we have such power is our goal. Whenever we let our thoughts take control, it is simply because we have forgotten that we are in control. We have surrendered to our minds the authority to navigate our ships, when in fact it is only a tool that we use to navigate through life. In a sense, our minds is the satellite that we use to receive and send the signals we wish to send. That is simply it. We must be able to reaffirm this within ourselves.

To further understand and enlighten ourselves with the role of our minds in our lives, let us review everything we have discussed. To start with, when it comes to choosing our self-identity, isn't it that it is our thoughts or ideas about who we are that influences it? Hence our self-identity is basically programmed through our minds. Using our awareness, we can choose to direct our minds to choose a certain idea over another. So, if we are choosing between the idea of the body and the idea of the soul as a foundation for our sense being, we have to do so through our minds. That being so, if we are unaware of this, our mind, without our permission, automatically chooses this for us. Which means, our mind takes the role of the leader whenever we let unawareness govern us. Further accentuating on the importance of having awareness in our lives. If we mindlessly let our own minds decide for us, we become a stranger even to ourselves. The mind, in a way, is the vice-captain who assumes responsibility for ourselves whenever we fail to become responsible for our own ship.

And whether we have a hateful, inconsiderate, unforgiving, and fearful vice-captain, or a self-loving, self-compassionate, forgiving, courageous one of course entirely depends on our supervision. Now being aware of the consequences of letting our minds get the best of us. Let us now figure out a way for us to reclaim control over our minds and ultimately over the entirety of our lives, and that is through meditation. A lot of people may have different descriptions as well as methods as to how it should be done, but the simplest way around the concept of meditation is plainly to cultivate awareness. And the easiest way for one to do that is to simply becoming aware of the most fundamental process that connects us to life, our breaths.

Now, our main focus for this chapter is to accentuate the fact that breathing consciously promotes and cultivates our awareness. Perhaps this is not the first book related to meditation that you have read, then this will not be the first time that you've heard such information. Think of it this way, oxygen from the air we breathe is practically the fuel that we use to operate our minds. Maybe you are thinking, what about the food we eat? Well, let's just say the food that we ingest is more for our body, not our minds. Moving on, the more oxygen that we inhale then the more aware we become, hence improving our chances at achieving control over ourselves, especially our thoughts. From the term itself, "conscious breathing", it is urgently suggested that we become more conscious and to put more attention to our breathing. Most of the time, if you haven't noticed it yet, something that also went unnoticed by me for years, or something I haven't really given importance to until I was made aware of it, is the fact that we do actually breathe mechanically. Breathing being an involuntary action, it continues to go on even if we are not conscious of it. Thereby, actively involving one's self in breathing we become more aware and grounded to what is happening to us intrinsically. This gives us more capacity to catch and stop ourselves whenever we are thinking about a certain negative thought which could potentially become the cause to us transitioning into an unfavorable mood. Also, consciously breathing, we learn to detach ourselves from the thoughts we are thinking, due to this, we are able to create space between our awareness and our thoughts. Doing so, we become significantly much more effective at stopping and redirecting our thoughts and our consciousness.

Meditation aswell grounds us into the present which allows us to see and be aware of the things that are already available to us. Being present connects us to the abundance that is already within our grasp, which are already available to us. Being connected to the present, we are most connected to reality. We are able to appreciate readily the concrete blessings that we already have. The oxygen that we breathe in itself is already very much a blessing for us. Which is one of the most symbolic things that we may relate to meditation. Meditation being an activity that improves our connection with our breath, with the oxygen that we inhale, it basically signifies our deep connection with life in itself. Breathing consciously, we exercise our most basic right of control. Doing so, we also allow space for silence to be cultivated within our thoughts. Which simply is the most important thing that meditation does for us. As this silence becomes the reference point for us to be able to achieve higher degrees of mindfulness. And it is exactly through this space of silence that we are able to contemplate on the many things regarding our self-awareness, our self-identity, and practically everything that we have discussed and are going to discuss in this book.

As we have mentioned in a previous part of this book, we are going to need lots of time to contemplate and reflect on the things we need to figure out. Meditating regularly helps us speed up that process. Imagine, as we consciously breathe in and breathe out, we also become increasingly conscious of not just our breathing but also everything that happens around us and within us, of course, our thoughts included. As we consciously breathe, our focus dwells mainly on the act of observation hence making us very sensitive and alert, hence, during this state, we get to watch over our thoughts with much greater ease. It would be as if we are watching a movie, as we are letting our thoughts drift through in right in front of us, with us simply observing these thoughts that arises and passes through. This way, we simply become a watcher of our thoughts, and through this, we cultivate our awareness of our thoughts, and from this space of awareness, we are then going to be more successful at catching ourselves thinking of an undesirable thought. Which, of course, being highly sensitive and alert to the thoughts that come and go, consequently we become more capable of redirecting them when needed. From this space of awareness, as we breathe in and out all the more consciously, we are going to be able to contemplate and ruminate through our thoughts from a more relaxed state of being. And as we practice more and more, we find it a lot easier to do so. Giving us more control over our thoughts, and gradually over our emotions, and so on and so forth. We become infinitely more calm and composed and in control of ourselves. Our minds are no longer left unsupervised as we are now more in control of ourselves and so we become more inclined towards peace. Which is the truest standard of a rational being.

Speaking of rationality, now let us also discuss about meditation as a method of surrender. For the first part of this chapter we discussed how meditation, in relation to conscious breathing, achieves for us a much higher quality of inner control or self-discipline. This time we are going to discuss how meditation can be used to do the opposite, but this time in terms of our control of the outside world. How many times have we frustrated ourselves or struggled profusely over just because of the actions of the people or basically the world around us? A lot of times, or maybe even every single day of our lives, isn't it not? Although, yes, we have also had our glorious moments in terms of events related to people or situations pleasing us, but overall, certain people or events will always find its way into displeasing us, no matter what we do. Unless of course we do not care what other people do or what happens around us. We surrender to the fact that people or situations will always manage to arouse a negative response from us which consequently is what makes it lose its power over us. Simply because when we surrender to such fact, we let go of our idea of control towards people and situations. Which is the main reason why we get frustrated over people or situations not following what we want. We take it against them for not following what we want. Which is impossible. Perhaps up to a certain extent we are able to control people or situations but this will never be so for all the time. People in positions of higher authority or power have a harder time accepting this fact because they are more used to being in control. Which is also what makes them significantly more frustrated whenever things do not go their way. Hence, the simplest solution, to surrender, to let go, not everything is within our control. Hence, for this, we must utilize meditation. Whenever we are faced with difficult people or events, always the best thing to do is to take a deep breath, first to be fully conscious of ourselves, and secondly for us to be able to remain calm. Being able to act composed during such times, is always the best thing we can do to achieve the most favorable outcome. How many times have we let our emotions or actions run rampant during extremely difficult situations that instead of being able to find resolve we find that we made the situation worse than it started.

Hence, we come back to the idea of self-control. In the end, it is only ourselves that we are truly in control of. To fantasize with the idea of being in control of people or situations is completely irrational. We have to accept the fact that we are never going to have full control over external things. If that is so then we wouldn't have to go through any problem in life, which would make it actually kind of boring. Life is simply not designed that way. Hence, we have foreshadowed that being able to surrender is an act of rationality. Although we surrender our power for external control, it is highly compensated as we generate and direct all our focus towards being able to control ourselves. This way, we will never get frustrated considering that if we have achieved a high level of control over ourselves, then we will not only be in control over our actions but also our thoughts and emotions. Hence, we acquire the capability to always be calm and composed during any situation or any difficult person we may face in our life. Which becomes the ultimate foundation to which we are going to base our peace from. Paradoxically, the act of letting go is the highest act of control. Letting go of control as the truest manifestation of power. This is what we achieve through meditation, through constant practice of conscious breathing, through consistent persistency to cultivate awareness. Our fate, handed to us in the palm of our hands, one of the highest forms of self-fulfillment one can achieve in a lifetime.

What is a positive mind?

Do you know that all things in this universe including thoughts are energy particles? If you think positively, the universe will match your energy and thoughts by bringing you a positive outcome. Therefore, it is very important for you to never fall prey to the negative spiral and self-doubting thoughts. Because whatever you think in life becomes your self-fulfilling prophecy.

A positive mind always thinks and visualizes about the best possible outcome for any situation, while a negative mind sinks only in misery and despair. This can be best explained by the following story:

The 2 wolves within

There is a story about an old man who teaches his little grandson a very important lesson of life.

He asked his grandson, "There are two wolves within all of us and they are always at battle with each other. One wolf represents all the good things in life such as joy, kindness, compassion, love, truth and hope. Whereas the other one is anger, evil, hate, lies and hopelessness. Which wolf do you think wins?"

Confused, the child replies, "I don't know grandfather, which one wins?"

His grandfather wisely smiles at him and gives him the most important lesson of his life. One that would build and shape his character forever.

"The one that you feed son."

This story applies to our mindsets. If we feed our minds positivity, then we can conquer the highest mountains in life. But if we feed our dark side, then we will never be able to reach anywhere in life.

Conditioned minds

It's not always your fault if you end up having a negative mindset. Society, parents, friends and the media all play their role towards that. You get told every day that something is impossible to achieve or attain and you end up thinking that for the rest of your life. It is your responsibility to break off these shackles that bind you to conformity and mediocrity.

The power of the subconscious mind

Your mind is divided into two portions: the conscious and the subconscious. While we are only aware of what our thoughts and feelings are when we are awake, the subconscious mind is working 24/7 and absorbing everything. When psychologists try to help people with their limiting beliefs, they are always trying to tap into the mind on the subconscious level.

The sub-conscious mind is very powerful, and in fact controls the conscious mind on the surface. All our deepest thoughts, feelings, desires and fears reside here. Therefore, even if you consciously try to suppress a thought or feeling, know that it stems from the subconscious and it is not going to go away until you address it and try to resolve it.

The subconscious mind never stops working and you find answers to all of your problems by tapping in its potential. The subconscious mind is very strong and you can't alter its thinking by simply using willpower. In fact it is the part of the brain that controls your conscious, so whatever feelings or thoughts that you are experiencing now, chances are they are stemming from the subconscious.

Whatever you experience on a conscious level gets recorded in the subconscious mind even if you literally don't remember it.

In order to change your mindset, you need to go to the core and start taking care of your subconscious mind because it also controls the body. This is why many people develop illnesses because they have stress and anxiety. Constantly thinking about negative events or experiences affects the body in various ways.

If you nurture your mind (both consciously and subconsciously) you will see a positive result in your life. You will heal easily, your mood will be better and you will attract other positive things in your life.

Suffering is a state of mind, no more no less. Specifically, one that involves thinking that we are losing something as of the moment. Losing something in the sense that we are focused on what we do not have instead of what we do have in life. A behavior that is highly connected to our natural tendency for survival, or more commonly known as our survival instinct. Of course, as a defense mechanism to anything that potentially endangers our well-being. Which, as we can see, has got a lot to do with declining resources. Resources which can come down to the most basic necessities in life; food, water, and air. Imagine, for example, a man trapped in a cave, gradually losing air to breathe, heavily panicking as he notices his body and mind slowly getting weaker because of the lack of oxygen circulating in his system. Panicking, as a definite reminder that without air to breathe, he is inevitably going to die, and so, he suffers. But apart from our basic needs, we also have higher needs. Which also translates to our needs which is beyond our physical needs. For having nourished the body, we then look for things that nourish our soul, our emotions. For example, our fascination towards listening to music. We look for music knowing that it inspires a pleasant emotion within us.

Suffering then, has also got a lot to do with our desires. Contemplating on the fact that these resources that we need in life are things that we desire for ourselves. Considering their importance to our overall well-being, we cannot help but desire these things whether or not they are truly a necessity in our lives as long as we get a certain kind of satisfaction from whatever it is that we desire. Of course, we cannot be afraid of losing something that we do not desire in the first place. We cannot grieve over something that we do not value. Isn't it that we could care less over losing something that we do not value in the first place?

But this instinct of ours does not necessarily need to invoke suffering. We suffer because we hold on to what our instinct tells us. We linger on to the thought that we are losing something when all we have to do is to view it as a guide. Our instinct may say that we are losing something but that doesn't mean we should react to it in an overwhelmingly negative manner, such as panicking for example. Instead, we can just be thankful that we are aware. For simply being aware of a negative situation, we are then capable of counteracting the situation by finding ways on how to prevent it from getting worse.

Going back to our self-identification. If we are identified with our bodies, certain events would have deep effects towards us. Such as losing material things. But if we are identified simply with our awareness, amazingly, many events in life that would seem devastating to most would seem trivial to us. Since, our personalities being rooted to our awareness, our desires also are greatly reduced, or in another sense, we become significantly detached from our desires. Considering the fact that as awareness, simply being alive or aware is already a lot for us. As awareness, it doesn't take a lot for us to become fully satisfied, and so we are incredibly low-maintenance beings. Being identified as awareness then, there is much little motivation to suffer. As opposed to being identified with the body, we have to have so many material things just for us to be satisfied, and so we become high-maintenance beings. For this we can suffer greatly.

Suffering then, involves a state of being in which we are too attached or too identified with the things that we are or the things that we have. Being greatly attached to these things, we react with a lot of displeasure even at the mere possibility of losing them. Hence, we must not hold on to these things so desperately or else we are indeed going to suffer. We must learn then how to take all things lightly, more so as an act of self-love and self-compassion. We acknowledge for suffering for what it is and let go of it. Looking back on the things that we have discussed so far, our suffering particularly stems from our attachment towards negative things such as hate. Hence the importance of all that we have discussed up to this point. Such as our self-identity, self-awareness, self-love, and forgiveness. These things basically point towards the things that we want and need in life, as well as the things we do not want and need. And these things that we do not want and need, to simplify, are basically those things that makes us suffer.

So with all that so far, what we have discussed, is the fact suffering is not entirely caused by the situations that are happening to us, but more so the thinking that we have during these situations. Articulating suffering in this manner, we find in ourselves a much greater understanding on how we are going to avoid and more so completely rid ourselves of it. Which is of course simply to change our thinking about a certain situation. To give a good example, think of the times that we are complaining about a certain event in our life. Let's say, we are complaining about how our bills become more and more expensive. When we are doing so, we are focusing on the idea that we are losing more money because our bills are becoming more expensive. Hence, we suffer. But instead, if we were to think that thankfully we have a job, and basically we have our gifts and talents that we may use so that we may be able to acquire the money that we need to pay these ever increasing bills, then we become more positive about the situation. When we focus on what we lose, indeed we lose, but if we focus on what we have, we thereby gain more of these things.

In this way, suffering then becomes a choice. We either focus on what makes us suffer or on what makes us not suffer. That ultimately, getting ourselves out of suffering is our responsibility, and is most definitely within our power. A lot of times we think that we are helpless towards these situations but that can be no more further from the truth. One of the noblest goals of this book is to slowly but surely give you back that power, and if you have already done so, strengthen that power even more. Which is what we have been basically nurturing so far. As we are becoming more self-aware, more self-compassionate, and more forgiving, we gradually acquire more power to have more self-control and inclination towards less suffering. For as we have declared, what we want most is to have more and more peace which in its most ideal sense also means virtually less and less suffering. With this thought, having learned about the mechanics of suffering, we are more capable of doing so. Peace, we are learning now, is more a matter of choice, a matter of deciding that we do not want suffering.

The Way to a Positive Mindset

Self-Acceptance

The first step to a healthy and positive mindset is to accept yourself no matter what. It doesn't matter what your skin color, weight or gender is because you are not a tiny little box that someone ticks based on the demographic you belong to. You are much more than that. You have the power to move mountains in life, yet like most people, you end up struggling with just tiny hills. So don't let your insecurity whatever it maybe hold you back from doing anything in life.

Love and accept every part of yourself and project it onto the world so that you get the same in return. Treat yourself kindly before anyone else does.

Practice Affirmations

This is a really important part of the process. Affirmations are statements and declarations one says, thinks or writes about oneself, in order to train the mind to think positively.

Once we start believing it, our subconscious mind is going to absorb it as well.

Positive affirmations are instrumental in developing a more confident and strong mind. You use them every day in different forms so that they get embedded deep within your mind.

Start by saying a few positive things about yourself and your life. You can either say it in front of a mirror or write it down in a journal. Whatever works for you as long as you do it every day.

E.g., you can say "I have an amazing life and I can do whatever I can."

"I am beautiful, and I have a lovely body."

"I love my family and friends."

These are just examples and of course you can customize your own affirmations. You can write positive quotes and stick them on your workstation or mirror as well so that your mind reads it every day and eventually accepts it. We become what we think about.

Positive affirmations help you attract all the things that you mention in them easily. This is also just like the Law of Attraction.

Practice Gratitude

Another crucial element of a positive mind is gratitude. You need to be thankful for all the things that you have been blessed with in life. These could be from the very little and mundane to the big and complex things in life. Everything happens for a reason. The pain that you see today will be the blessing you see tomorrow.

That break-up you are heartbroken about is preparing you for a better love life with another loving and caring person. Getting fired from a job maybe a sign that you have a better career opportunity out there for you.

That illness you might have is here to tell you to value your health and help others who are struggling with the same illness. Our response to whatever happens to us is the final result of the experience we have in our life. So in essence there are no failures, just our actions or thoughts towards whatever happens to us.

We all have our battles and demons to fight with. They are not here to defeat us but to make us stronger and braver. It's hard but you have to be grateful and only then will you see positive things manifest into your life that you could never have imagined.

Surround yourself with positive people

One of the most important things that you can do is to interact more with positive people. Building a support system encourages you is vital in helping you achieve your goals and ambitions. Avoid engaging with toxic or negative people who'll only bring you down.

If you want to make better friendships then join different clubs or meet-up groups and build new connections with likeminded people.

Studies show that people who have an active and healthy social life tend to neither get less sick nor suffer from feelings of depression. The feeling of isolation is very frustrating so always have some good friends with you that you can interact with on a regular basis.

Be aware of your thoughts

Most of the time people have their thoughts running on default and they are not mindful of them. This means that there is no filter to stop any negative thoughts and so it is really easy for them to fall prey to the vicious cycle of negativity. It might seem quite difficult to put a filter on your thoughts but with a little practice you can become more of a conscious person when thinking about things. This is definitely not to say to stop or suppress your thoughts because that is almost impossible. But to change the way you feel about things when you see or experience them.

See the positive in everything

You don't have to be a Pollyanna and pretend to be happy when life is difficult. But your response should be towards tackling every situation and doing something about it. Only then will things start improving and changing the course of their direction.

This also includes seeing the good in others as well. Try to see the good in everyone because this will prevent you from having any negative biases or perceptions about others. Compliment others because who knows you might end up making someone else's day wonderful.

Spread positivity around

The best way to be more positive is to spread it around others as well.

Smile—research shows that smiling makes the brain release endorphins and serotonin that help relax the body and mind. Smiling is infectious as well and you will notice a positive response 99% of the time whenever you smile at someone.

Do volunteer work—helping the less fortunate will make you count your blessings in life and be more grateful.

Play with children and pets—they are the most innocent beings that that you can easily make happy. You will appreciate the little joys in life that come from playing with them.

Donate—give away things you don't need to people who do. It could be old clothes, books or even money.

Meditate

Meditation has been proven to reduce stress and anxiety from people's life. You don't necessarily have to join a yoga class to be good at meditating. You can meditate in a quiet room in as little as 10 minutes a day. Just set some time aside for yourself and clear your mind of all the clutter and worries that make you feel all anxious or angry.

Breathe deeply and close your eyes. Focus on just being relaxed and happy. Once you start doing this regularly, you can even increase the time of your meditation and it won't seem uncomfortable or strange to you anymore.

No more surviving, it's time for thriving!

Whatever you have experienced in life, it is time to move past it and stop using the victim card. Positive people even if they are victims to circumstances, don't just sit there and blame others or life for their misery.

You can change your life if you just put your mind to it but it will only happen if you stop carrying around the baggage of victimhood and self-pity. As harsh as it sound, nobody likes a pity party. People might feel bad for you for one day and try to help you but if all they see is you wallowing all the time and not do anything about it, they will start avoiding you and not feel bad for you anymore. Be an inspiration to others by thriving at life and not just surviving.

J. K Rowling, author of the tremendously popular Harry Potter books was a divorced single mother of a little baby boy, living in a rat infested apartment in one of the poorest areas of London. Rejected by 12 different publishers; she still didn't give up and was positive that she would get published. Eventually she got accepted and we all know the rest of the story.

Forgive others

The last step to having a positive mindset is to forgive people for their mistakes because nobody is perfect. Holding on to anger and resentment for what you experienced in the past burdens you forever. You end up walking around with so much pain and anger that it is impossible for you to have a peace of mind. At the end of the day forgiving someone is more about the sanity of your mind so forgive people and move on.

Having a positive mind is not that difficult once you move past these barriers that block you. It is also not possible to never be negative. The key is to maintain a healthy balance that is gravitating mostly towards the positive side.

Forgiving others does not mean that you are ok with what they did to you nor are you condoning any of their actions. It is simply another process of healing from the hurt you are going through. Most of the times people can't progress with their lives is because they haven't forgiven the people who wronged them.

Forgiveness also makes you a better person and helps you to be a more compassionate person. Even if the person didn't ask for forgiveness but you have to forgive for your sake.

Chapter 10

PUTTING YOURSELF INTO ACTION

One easy way to increase your self-love and your standard of life is by lavishing love and care on yourself. Taking adequate care of yourself, both physically and psychologically, will help you look and feel better, which will increase your-self love.

Here are some examples of how to take care of yourself:

1: Never miss your night sleep for anything

Always ensure you get adequate sleep. Sometimes you may be tempted to stay up, attend to certain issues, and catch up with sleep the next day. In as much as you can make up for the sleepless night, nothing compares to that good night sleep you missed.

The human body secretes hormones that signal the brain to shut down and rest during the night. Getting adequate sleep is a good way to improve your quality of life.

This usually leads to an all round healthier life which you can benefit from.

2: Engage in physical exercises

Physical exercise help keep your body healthy enough to serve you better. You can start with maybe joining a local gym, start cycling, taking part in a sport, taking regular long walks or maybe jogging. Exercise usually helps people clear their mind and feel good about themselves due to a sense of motivation and achievement.

In addition to ensuring that you stay fit and healthy, engaging in physical exercise can do so many things for you. In fact, coupled with a good weight-management diet plan, physical exercises are one of the surest ways to lose weight and keep away the unwanted weight.

3: Mind what you eat

This piece of advice is one most of us do not want to hear. Most of us want to eat whatever catches our fancy and whatever we crave. Someone once said that you are what you eat.

If there is one thing that ensures you live a good life for as long as you live, it is insistence on nothing but natural organic clean foods and avoiding processed junk. Eating good can usually have a positive effect on you, making you feel good about yourself and life in general.

There are several ways you can give yourself special treats similar to those you would give to someone you love. Here are ways of treating yourself

Occasionally pamper yourself

Pampering yourself involves taking time off everything that keeps you busy so you can really concentrate on giving yourself some special treatments such as a sensual massage or visiting a spa center.

When it comes to increasing self-love, how you pamper and treat yourself can help improve how you see and how you feel about yourself as a whole.

When you do well, reward yourself

One easy way to develop self-love is to reward yourself whenever you achieve a milestone. Rewarding yourself helps you feel better and makes you want to succeed more and to prove to yourself that you have all it takes to succeed.

Set regular targets and decide what incentives/rewards you will give yourself each time you successfully achieve your target. Your target can range from cultivating a new habit to starting something you have been putting off for ages such as taking piano lessons, writing a new book, starting that small business, etc.

Whenever you achieve that feat, reward yourself by buying yourself that gift you want, taking yourself out to somewhere cool and fun to give yourself a special treat, hanging out with that special someone who makes you feel like you have no care in the world, etc.

It may not be easy to develop self-love if you do not change certain things about yourself that reduce your self-worth and self-respect. Certain factors can make you feel unworthy of anything.

When you change certain things about yourself, things that affect your self-esteem and how you see yourself, you will increase your self-love.

Here are some tips on things you can change in your life and increase self love:

Simplify your life

Many of us complicate things for ourselves by clustering our lives with things we can easily do without. When you take up more things than you can easily handle within the time and space available to you, you end up with several unfinished tasks and abandoned projects. The more you begin things and never finish them, and the more you leave things here and there half done, the more your self-confidence and self-respect decrease.

When you simplify your life by ensuring you take up only things you can easily handle, life becomes easier and more interesting since you have more time to focus on yourself and other very important issues in your life such as your family and relationship. The more time you have to concentrate on the things that really matter, the more you love the person you are.

But, how can you simplify your life? Here are some ideas:

Review your circle of friends

Let us be truthful, some people in your circle of friends should not be there. Certain people that occupy space in your life never make any meaningful contribution from year to year. Instead, such people are negative, never seem to encourage you and make you feel bad at yourself.

Evaluate your friends and decide which ones to keep and which ones to start spending less time with. People that cause you to do things that result in self-loathing should not be on your friends list. It is important to understand that to live a quality life; you do not need many friends. All you need is a handful that can bring out the best in you, help you overcome your negative habits, learn new positive habits, and believe in yourself and your ability to achieve all your goals.

Review your To-Do list

Several things on your daily To-Do list are things you can delete and not feel as if anything vital is missing from the list. Evaluate the activities you engage in and you spend a lot of time doing without getting much result and get rid of them. Consider the sitcoms and soap operas you spend hours watching at home and see how you can reduce the number of hours you spend watching them.

You need to understand that anything that does not help you get better will not increase your self-love and progression in life, therefore should not be a part of your life.

The fewer things you have to attend to, the more time you have to do things that improve your life and benefit you as a person, things such as learning new skills, reading new books and joining new causes.

Become a Minimalist

Minimalism is all about living with less and still feeling fulfilled. Becoming a minimalist entails reducing the amount of stuff you have in your home/office such as your clothing, papers, books, electronics, etc. Minimalism can also involve moving from a big home to a smaller one.

A smaller home means you have to live with fewer belongings that require less time and resources to maintain. The extra time you would have spent maintaining a big home is time you can use to pursue other things that can improve your life.

Self-Compassion & Relationships

The importance of relations in everybody's life cannot be denied. The human relationships and social structure is quite impressive and distinguishes us from other species. A relation can be with your relatives, guy friend or a girl friend. It is good to maintain healthy relationship with people close to you in order to gain trust and acceptance. In healthy relationships you are not isolated, you can share your views and thoughts and ask for advice. Apart from this the quality of relationships that you have with others also affects our physical and mental health.

Like its effects on other spheres of life, self-compassion, relations and the personal life of the person are also interlinked. Self-compassionate people are more happy, caring, supportive and accepting in their relations. Such people grant more autonomy and freedom to their partners and close ones. They have the tendency to share their perspective, thought and ideas with their close ones. Such people also lead a good life, because they are able to share the happenings in their lives and release off some burden.

Relationships are affected greatly by even small acts of compassion. Self-compassion and compassion with others give us more personal control, loving nature and confidence. When we have control over ourselves we know about our limits and our abilities, and we work and cooperate with others according to our capacities. Loving nature is equally important in any sort of relation. It can make us supportive and caring towards other people in our lives. Confidence is also something which matters the most in relations, if you want to have perfect communication and understanding with others, confidence might be the right key.

Lack of self-compassion can lead a person to rejection sensitivity in their relationships. As described earlier rejection sensitivity in relationships is often a problem that needs to be addressed either on your own or by consulting a specialist, before it is too late. The rejection sensitive people lead a problematic life and they usually perceive and think negatively about the outcome of their relations. The chances of such people to engage in constructive communication are very less. Apart from this they might actually self-silence themselves. Self-silencing might help such people momentarily in escaping from the realities, but eventually the negative outcomes will start to appear in your relationships. The way out from the problem of rejection sensitivity is to practice self-compassion, to get rid of their complexes.

Self-compassion and compassion are also helpful in romantic relationships. Two people who display self-compassion for themselves almost automatically generate compassion for the other spouse because of their optimism and space they provide for their other partner in every aspect of life. They do not employ criticism or rudeness or being biased for solving their problems, they are calm and as the communication gap in them is very less so they solve their matters with harmony. In this way they make better spouses than people who show little or no compassion.

Professional relations with customers, other organizations and among the staff itself are also important. In has been noted that people who regularly receive and practice compassion while at work; voluntarily or involuntarily, have a good response towards their tasks and their capacities are enhanced. They see their organization, their colleagues and themselves in a positive light. They feel positive emotions like contentment and joy, moreover their commitment with their job is noteworthy.

There is no surprise in the fact that people who make use of self-compassion are the ones who have compassion for other people in their lives. The compassionate people instead of ignoring the sufferings of others tend to notice and acknowledge them and then try their best to alleviate their pain with warmth, kindness and understanding. They do not consider the physical, monetary or social situation of the affected fellow, rather they try to recognize what they have in common with them. Moreover, according to experts in order to get an idea of what self-compassion is like, it is quite helpful to see compassion in other people around you. So the compassionate people can lead the way by setting an example of compassion for others to follow.

Maintaining Self Compassion

After having a thorough look at the benefits of self-compassion, our major concern now maintaining it. At first doing self-compassion might take some courage and seem unnatural. Some individuals might find it difficult, especially people who have recently experienced trauma, so in some case to get a kick start you need some psychologist or a therapist, who might help you begin from somewhere. The strategies discussed in this chapter will considerably help you in maintaining self-compassion.

Consider How You Would Treat Someone Else

This actually might be the simplest solution to maintain self-compassion. Imagine that someone close to you got rejected or failed and came to you. How would you treat that person? What are the words that you would say? Which words you would not like to say to them? Certainly you will take an initiative to encourage or motivate them, so that they can overcome their problems and start their normal life. Similarly it is quite effective in maintaining self-compassion when you treat your own self in the same way as you treat your close ones.

Watch Your Language Before reading this book you might have been in habit of criticizing yourself without realizing it. So it might be quite useful to pay attention to the words that you speak to your own self in or after difficult situations. Try not to say some to yourself which you would not like to say to someone beloved, if you are doing otherwise then certainly it should be termed as self-criticism and it is well established that self-criticism is a major hindrance in your path to success.

Comforting Oneself with Physical Gestures

It is a well known fact that kind and caring gestures have a quick effect on our operating abilities and our body itself. Such positive gestures activate your soothing parasympathetic system. In some cultures, it is said that kind and caring gestures toward oneself drop you in your body from your head, because the head does not want to stick with the storyline and loves to deny realities because of the human instinct. While the body stands for the place where you get comfort and you are away from emotion. In this regard any gesture can work, but the gestures of putting your hand on your heart and holding your arm, patting on your own shoulder or massaging your temples are quite effective.

Memorizing Compassionate Phrases

The maintenance of self-compassion in the time of adversities might seem to be a challenge but you can take deep breaths, gently put one of your hands on your heart and repeat the phrases below:

> This is moment of suffering

> Suffering is a part of life

> May I be kind to myself

> May I give myself the compassion I need

These phrases include the essence of all the three discussed components of self compassion that have been described in chapter 1. The first phrase gives the message of being mindful of the sufferings. The second phrase tells us that all human beings have to go through sufferings so there is nothing to be ashamed of when you are in trouble. The third phrase compels us leave self-criticism and hold fast to self-compassion. The last phrase gives us the message that our own self is in dire need of self-compassion so we deserve it the most in situation of adversity. This practice is a sort of mediation and it is observes that talking to oneself or doing meditation at times can be effective in controlling emotions and being rational.

Self-compassion Diary

Try to keep a self-compassion diary for a time period you like. Writing a diary can help you in expressing your own emotions to yourself and it contributes in well-being both emotionally and physically. Write about the things that made you feel sad, ashamed or stressed. As you are writing don't try to be judgmental of your experiences. In the end write some words in a reassuring tone that might comfort you. In the end of the day read it again. Keeping a diary will surely help you in organizing your own thoughts and translate them for compassion towards yourself.

Morning Rituals

Try to make it a habit to do a morning ritual everyday. Consider yourself fortunate that your have woken up and you are alive and breathing. Reflect on the importance of your life and make a commitment to yourself, that you will not waste it and try the best to develop yourself and expand your feeling not only to yourself but also others around you. Surely you can add more thoughts to the ritual that you are going to practice. This will automatically help you be more self-compassionate towards yourself throughout the day and its effects on compassion towards others will also be noteworthy.

Practice Acts of Kindness

Now if you have practiced all this you would certainly love to enjoy everyday acts of kindness towards yourself and the people around you. If you see yourself in some distress show some empathy towards yourself, if someone else is suffering try to solve their problem and make them happy. Even if someone has hurt you a bit which affected you, and you have them in mind, try to forgive that person and look forward to having a good relation with them. Ultimately all of this would help you in your aim of developing self-compassion, because when we have compassion for others we get to know their situation and what they might be thinking and what do they want. Similarly when you are having problems you would also do the same for yourself.

Self-compassion through Writing

Writing can also help you in your efforts for self-compassion. The writing exercise can be broken down into three parts:

- ❖ Ponder over the imperfections that make you feel down.
- ❖ From the view point of a loving friend, write a supposed letter to yourself.
- ❖ Feel the compassion comforting and soothing you.

Everyone is not perfect and has imperfections that make them feel insecure, feeling of shame and inadequate. In the first step write about the issues that give you a feeling of inadequacy. What are the emotions that surface when you think about those issues? Try to feel your emotions and then write them down in words.

In the second step think about a best friend of yours who knows all your weaknesses and strengths, including the issues that you wrote earlier. Ponder over what you think your friend might think of you and how that friend loves you with all your shortcomings and imperfections. This friend knows the limits of the nature of humans and is quite forgiving towards you. Now try writing a letter to yourself from the view point of that good friend and try to focus on what that friend will tell you in the moment of despair and how they would convey the compassion that they feel towards you. Also think of possible suggestion your friend would give to you.

After writing the letter put it aside for a while and rest for a few minutes. Now read it again and enjoy the comfort it gives to you in the form of compassion. Literally you would feel the compassion being showered on you.

Conclusion

One thing you need to pay attention to, something that will help you love yourself more and treat yourself with greater respect, is your level of confidence. Self-confidence is one attribute that makes you daring enough to believe you can succeed where and when everyone thinks you will surely fail.

Have you seen a smaller boxer taking on an obviously bigger opponent and winning the contest and wondered what gave him the guts to challenge the giant? Only self-confidence borne of self-belief and respect can drive a man to challenge what is obviously greater than he is and come out victorious.

How can you grow your level of self-confidence so you can dare more, win more, love yourself more, and live more?

Here are some ideas to help you:

Go places you have always avoided

Fear is the major reason why you have a low level of confidence or lack self-confidence entirely. The best way to conquer your fears is to do the very thing you fear. To do this, come up with a list of things you fear and rate them 1 to 10 with 1 being less fearful, and 10 being most fearful.

Start doing the things you fear beginning with the ones, you fear less. As you tackle what you don't fear most, you will grow confidence to deal with the things you feel the most, and one day, you will be amazed that you have overcome doing things you never thought you could do.

Whenever you attempt something scary and succeed, you naturally raise the love, respect, and belief you have in yourself.

For example, if you fear public speaking, you will always feel inferior because you cannot speak out when and where most of your peers are speaking. However, the day you learn to dare that fear and damn the consequences, you will notice an improvement in how you see yourself, which will help you dare more, achieve more, love the new more daring you, and live a better life.

Take up challenging tasks

If you keep taking tasks that are within your qualification and expertise, you may not be able to build the right level of self-confidence needed to attain your dreams. Sometimes you need to defy all odds and attempt the things everyone says are impossible. You may not achieve success on every venture you set out to achieve, but you will at least become more fearless and courageous to try other such things in future.

The more you build your courage, the more you develop self-love. The more self-love you develop, the higher your chances of living a fulfilled life. That task in your industry, organization, community or school that requires someone bold enough to go out on a limb to save the situation should be an opportunity for you to raise your level of confidence and self worth. When others shy away and give reasons why they cannot, find a reason why you can and do it to prove a point to yourself.

Well I hope you enjoyed this book and it gave you plenty of value. It would be a great help if you left us a review telling us what you thought of the book.

www.ingramcontent.com/pod-product-compliance
Lightning Source LLC
Chambersburg PA
CBHW081228080526
44587CB00022B/3858